Surviving the
Terrible Teens

Surviving the
Terrible Teens
How to have a teenager and stay sane

Dr Sandi Mann, Dr Paul Seager and Jonny Wineberg

Editor: Roni Jay

WHITE
LADDER
PRESS
new tricks for old dogs

Published by White Ladder Press Ltd

Great Ambrook, Near Ipplepen, Devon TQ12 5UL

01803 813343

www.whiteladderpress.com

First published in Great Britain in 2008

10 9 8 7 6 5 4 3 2

13-digit ISBN 978 1 905410 25 5

British Library Cataloguing in Publication Data

A CIP record for this book can be obtained from the British Library.

Designed and typeset by Julie Martin Ltd
Cover photos by Jonathon Bosley
Cover design by Julie Martin Ltd
Printed and bound by TJ International Ltd, Padstow, Cornwall
Cover printed by St Austell Printing Company

Printed on totally chlorine-free paper
The paper used for the text pages of this book is FSC certified.
FSC (The Forest Stewardship Council) is an international
network to promote responsible management of the world's forests.

FSC
Mixed Sources
Product group from well-managed
forests and other controlled sources

Cert no. SGS-COC-2482
www.fsc.org
© 1996 Forest Stewardship Council

White Ladder books are distributed in the UK by Virgin Books

White Ladder Press
Great Ambrook, Near Ipplepen, Devon TQ12 5UL
01803 813343
www.whiteladderpress.com

Contents

Acknowledgements

We would like to thank the hundreds of parents who took part in our research for this book; many thanks for completing the questionnaires and sharing your experiences. We would like to make special mention of the members of our Parents Panel for taking the time and trouble to read an earlier draft of this book and for giving us their comments and feedback. They are:

Helen Eastham of Preston
Janet Tideswell of Newcastle-under-Lyme
Abigail Escreet of Manchester
Bev Hall of Preston
Carole Knight of Longridge, Lancashire
Glenys Duce of Nottingham,
Karyn Bishop of Welling, Kent
Heather Wicks of Penn, Buckinghamshire
Joy Pettitt of Portslade, Brighton

Comments from members of the Parents Panel

"*Surviving the Terrible Teens* is really accessible and useful. I particularly liked the exercise about identity with the 10 questions, which I found started some interesting conversations with my teenage son."

"I found the book extremely helpful on how to deal with many areas of teenage angst. I found the chapter on understanding your teenager the best one of all – knowing when to press for answers and when to leave them alone is very useful advice. Also, understanding that I'm not failing as a parent if I don't know everything about my son."

"I found *Surviving the Terrible Teens* very interesting, readable and humorous in places. I feel parents will connect with many elements of the book and think 'Yes, that's just how it is!' I feel the book is a useful tool which will help parents look from another perspective."

"I thought it was pretty good overall, an easy to read information text that parents could dip in and out of and refer to specific things as needed."

"I have enjoyed reading it, very much. There were points when I actually wished I had been given the opportunity to read it six years ago."

"I found the style easy and flowing. The information and language used is accessible, understandable and results in the reader being able to connect with the flow of the text through the chapters. You have managed to avoid academic linguistics which can be intimidating and a turn-off especially in a subject like this. However, the standard of the information, discussions and theories is clearly high. I found myself nodding and agreeing and laughing and pondering. This really does make a good handbook for having a teen – I liked the fact that the style encouraged me to become part of the process I was reading as opposed to being told that this is how my teen behaves or behaved. I liked it a lot."

"I think the book is really useful and has many ideas for parents to consider."

"I think this book is going to become my bible!"

Dedications

From Sandi

For my parents, for all the trials and tribulations they
endured during my (long-gone!) teenage years.

From Paul

To Holly: thanks for your unending love and support – with
all my love as always.

To my Mum & Dad with love: you were naturals when it
came to bringing up a teen – I seem to have turned out all
right! Thank you.

From Jonny

For my wife, the mother of my future teenagers, for putting
up with my inner-teenager for all these years.

About the authors

Although **Dr Sandi Mann** is a 'workplace' psychologist at the University of Central Lancashire, her background in youth-related issues often enables her to combine her interests with working with teenagers. She has a Masters Degree in Child and Adolescent Psychology and is former Chair of a youth project in Manchester. She has conducted two major research projects on identifying the needs of teenagers for a regional charity and has been involved in research on sex education in schools for a national charity. Sandi currently conducts training in schools for teenagers on stress management, assertion skills, communication skills and anger management.

Dr Paul Seager is a psychologist at the University of Central Lancashire who specialises in the area of social psychology including topics such as social influence (including peer pressure), group identity, deception and conformity issues. He has worked with teenagers, delivering a number of training courses, including anger management and improving communication skills.

Jonny Wineberg is a consultant working with children's and youth organisations, advising them on the diverse issues that affect them. Formerly deputy principal youth officer for Manchester City Council, he is also a visiting lecturer in youth work at Nazarene Theological College, convenes the Faith

Youth Groups forum for Manchester and sits on the Manchester Youth Matters board. He has delivered training for hundreds of youth workers and young people on many issues including bullying, eating disorders, drug awareness, communication skills and sexual health both in the UK and abroad, including France, Australia and the USA.

Introduction

"Living with a teen is like treading on eggshells. Things can get pretty heated if you say the wrong thing. They regard parents as the ultimate embarrassment and will not want to be seen with you. But, generally it's great!" *Parent of 13 year old boy*

"It is very difficult to live with someone who is an absolute delight one minute and like an alien from outer space the next. We sometimes think we are just a 'bad smell' to him." *Parent of 16 year old boy*

"Teenagers are growing up in a rapidly changing hyper-real world, far different than the one experienced by previous generations and even that of older siblings. We can no longer say 'We know how you feel' as our parents could." *Parent of a teenager*

When you become a new parent, there is no shortage of help and advice in the form of books and magazines, but somehow these seem to be rather thin on the ground once your child becomes school-aged. And, by the time you shakily embark on that perilous journey that being the parent of a teen entails, all those self-help and advice guides mysteriously disappear. Yet coping with teens is in many ways so much more demanding than handling even the most difficult of the baby and toddler stages. Sleepless nights return (due to worry or waiting up for errant teens to return home), tantrums re-emerge (and they are so much worse than the most challenging efforts by the terrible twos) and your home is once again filled with such conflict, tension and chaos that make the early years seem like a teddy bears' picnic in comparison.

It is not all bad by any means and the teen years can be a delightful time (when it is not hell on earth, of course). The aim of this book is to guide you through the turbulent years that we call the teens – to help you cope, to show you that you are not alone and to give you practical tips and guidance for dealing with your own particular brand of teen.

We have drawn on a wealth of psychological knowledge, theory, research and experience to best advise you but we have also taken great pains to incorporate the real-life experiences and viewpoints of parents who have done it all before you. To that end, we have canvassed the views of 170 parents of teenagers who have been there and got the T-shirt. We also set up a Parents Panel of nine parents who have read the entire book and passed comment on it before publication. All these views combine to make this book a unique and valuable investment for any parent of a teen.

We hope you enjoy this book, are reassured by it and find it a valuable guide to the sometimes difficult days that lie ahead. Our ultimate aim is to help you enjoy your teenager as much as possible; it really won't be too long (though far too long for some of you) before they become adults and leave home to embark on the next stage of their lives. Use this book to make the most of the teenage years – and to cope with the mess, noise, angst and attitude that are part and parcel of the whole experience. Just remember – you'll miss it all when they've moved on (maybe!).

About the research

We sent out hundreds of questionnaires to parents of teenagers, via national magazines (with thanks to Woman's Own), local newspapers and via company intranet mailings. We received 170 questionnaires of which 163 were complete (the incomplete ones were still useful for their comments). Slightly more boys were surveyed than girls – 55% of the questionnaires were about teenage boys compared with 45% about girls. We wonder whether parents of boys were more motivated to complete our surveys (perhaps because they experience more problems?) or whether this is just a statistical blip.

The age range that we surveyed was from 12 to 19 with roughly equal splits across the ages:

Age 12/13 – 16%
Age 14 – 13%
Age 15 – 21%
Age 16 –18%
Age 17 –11%
Age 18/19 – 21%

We didn't ask if it was the mother or the father who completed the questionnaire – the only requirement was that they were the child's parent or step-parent. It is likely that the majority were completed by mothers simply because of where we targeted our recruitment efforts (such as women's magazines) and because mothers are more likely to be the primary care-givers. Certainly, the vast majority of questionnaires that we sent out were addressed to women. Although this may influence some of the findings, we felt it appropriate for the main carer to be the one to complete the questionnaires.

Chapter 1

Who is this creature I spawned?

Teenagers today are moulded by a wide variety of influences, some of which you may be less than happy about. From pop stars to the latest reality TV wannabes, from football heroes to big-screen icons – all these may seem to hold more sway on your teen's rapidly developing mind than you ever could. Throw into the cauldron a liberal sprinkling of teen mags, a dash of computer games and a large measure of the latest cult DVDs, and you may be left wondering just what part, if any, you have to play in the development of your precious teen's fragile psyche. This chapter will examine all the influences, for good or bad, that your teen is likely to encounter – and how to throw your own values and beliefs into the mix to enable you to play a significant role in their emotional development.

Self-identity – who does your teen think they are?

Self-identity is the perception that we have of ourselves – whether we are kind, moral, political, whether we affiliate ourselves to a particular sports team, like a particular style of music, dress in a certain way – these all help form a sense of who we are. This self-identity develops through childhood: newborn babies do not see themselves as a separate entity from their mother – this sense of self develops as they come to realise that they are indeed a separate person. As they get older, children also realise that they can have separate feelings, likes and desires from their parents (a three year old might expect mum to like The Tweenies or cheese dipped in ketchup just because they do, whereas at seven they understand that they may be different from mum). By the teenage years, children may actively seek to develop a distinctive identity that distinguishes them clearly from their parents so as to reaffirm that they are indeed an independent and separate person. This is why teenage rebellion is rife as they may be driven to choose clothes, interests and values simply to assert their own unique identity.

How in touch are you with your teenager's developing sense of self? Do you know what their hopes are, their dreams, their fears? To understand your teen you have to know what drives them, what is important to them, and crucially, how they perceive themselves – this is all part of their self-identity. Take our quiz (see page 13) to see how in tune you really are. This is important because the more you know your teen, the better able you are to understand them.

"Completing the questionnaire made me realise how little I know my teenager. Like most teenagers, he is living in his own world with his friends and does not seem to want to engage to any extent with his parents." *Parent of 15 year old boy*

Self-identity quiz

Write down the answers to as many of the following questions as you can (if you can't answer any, you clearly need to get to know your teen better). Next, encourage your teen to answer the same questions and compare notes to see how in tune you are with their self-identity. This may also be a useful exercise for your teen in helping crystallise their self-identity.

- What three words would best describe your teen?
- What do they want to be when they 'grow up'?
- What is your teen frightened of?
- What does your teen worry about?
- How does your teen like to spend their spare time?
- What issues (e.g. political, environmental) concern them?
- Who is their current idol/hero?
- What is their best quality?
- What is their worst quality?
- List any groups to which your teen belongs

Each of the quiz questions has a specific purpose in helping to uncover your teen's self-identity. Choosing three words that best describes them helps focus on their most prominent traits – i.e. those that most strongly define them. Their career aspirations may reflect a deeper sense of who they want to be; for example, if they want to be a teacher, it might be because they aspire to help others and see themselves as a caring individual (as opposed to just wanting the long holidays...). Your teen's fears and worries may surprise you and reveal more about them than you realised; for example, worries about death may reflect a deep-seated fear of separation from you – or, alternatively, may simply be the result of worrying about stories they see in the media.

Belonging to groups is also an important element of self-identity. When we are faced with uncertain situations, we naturally look to others for clues as to how to behave (we call this Social Validation Theory). Teenagers are often faced with uncertain situations, simply because they are too inexperienced to know the 'rules'. For example, a teen who goes to a party on their own may be unsure about how to act. They look around, see a member of their football team and copy their behaviour.

All the issues touched on by these questions are fundamental to understanding and coping with your teenager so will be explored in more detail throughout the book.

Self-esteem – do they like who they are?

Self-esteem is a measure of our self-worth. It is different from self-identity (which is who we think we are) and from a related concept, that of self-efficacy (or self-confidence), which is a measure of how competent we think we are. However, our self-confidence can directly impact on our self-esteem – if we think we are poor at something that we value then our self-esteem is likely to be lowered.

Our survey said...

Parents of teenagers in our survey generally thought that their teens suffered from lack of self-confidence in several areas. The least self-confidence was felt in terms of coping

with romantic relationships: 54% of parents felt that their teens lacked confidence in this area; 30% felt that their teens lacked confidence in their academic ability with almost the same number (29%) lacking confidence in their appearance.

Self-esteem is vital for your teen's blossoming sense of self and having low self-esteem can be extremely damaging in the long term. Teenagers (and adults) with low self-esteem can have lowered expectations and thwarted ambition; they do not think that they are worthy of anything great so are less likely to try. Low self-esteem can also produce an individual who is anxious to please and impress others and finds it difficult to say No, making them very susceptible to peer pressure (see Chapter 2). Bullies sometimes have low self-esteem and may compensate for their low self-worth by trying to raise it at the expense of weaker others (see Chapter 6).

Could you be the cause of your teen's low self-esteem? Most parents would be horrified at this suggestion but ask yourself the following questions:

- Do you constantly criticise your teen?
- Do you contradict their ideas?
- Do you rubbish their dreams?
- Are you always saying 'no' to them?
- Do you unreasonably restrict their independence?
- Do you often fail to value their opinions?
- Do you rarely *really* listen to what they say?
- Do you fail to show an interest in their day-to-day life?
- Do they feel as though they don't have your support?
- Do you undermine them in front of their friends?

If any of these strikes a chord with you, then perhaps you're not doing your teen's self-esteem any favours. Of course low self-esteem can come from other sources so don't be too hard on yourself. For example, a teacher's criticism of their work, a friend's put-down about their appearance, a bad exam mark or an unfavourable self-comparison with a celebrity in a magazine – all these can have a constant and pernicious effect on the development of your teen's fragile self-esteem. Many of these will be discussed in greater detail in later chapters.

Bolstering your teen's self-esteem

OK, so perhaps their self-esteem isn't as high as it could be, but don't despair as there are some fairly simple techniques that you can use to bolster your teen's self-esteem.

If you need to criticise your teen (and the chances are you probably will), try to make sure that it is constructive as opposed to destructive criticism. Constructive criticism is acknowledging a fault, but giving them a way of improving, while destructive criticism is just pointing out the faults: for example, if they have done badly in an exam, constructive criticism would be to acknowledge that they haven't done as well as they might have done, and suggesting ways in which they might improve next time, such as revising more topics. Destructive criticism would be to berate your teen for not performing well.

If you are in the habit of dissing their ideas without giving them full consideration, perhaps you should take pause. You should be aware that their idea may be a good one if you gave them a chance to explain it. However, if you still think that their idea of leaving school to follow their pop idol round the world is not their best idea, then you probably need to take action. Instead of contradicting their idea out-of-hand, acknowledge the good points (they get to visit lots of interesting places), but then ask them open questions about what they need to reach their goal and *gently* point out the flaws in their argument (where do we start?). This will ensure that they don't become too defensive, which an outright contradiction may do, but instead leads them subtly to the conclusion that their idea isn't as good as they first thought it was.

Similarly, don't rubbish their dreams, reality check them instead. So, if your darling Poppy or Ethan dreams of being a popstar, astronaut or brain surgeon, get them thinking about what they will need to do to achieve this dream. One easy way to do this would be to engage their penchant for the internet (most teens seem to see use of this tool as their God-given right) and encourage them to search online for resources about their chosen profession. If you know anyone who is in that line of business, suggest that your teen drops them an email or even speaks to them on the phone. The bottom line here is not to dismiss their dream out of hand but to get them to think about the nuts and bolts that are used to construct the dream – and if this means some other source rubbishing their dream, better that than you.

LIAM'S STORY

"Our son, Liam, who was 14 at the time, dreamt of being an actor. At first we didn't take it seriously and kept telling him to concentrate on his studies so he could get himself a 'proper' job when he left school. His drama teacher, however, got him to research how to actually become an actor. Liam went on the internet and discovered that he needed to go to university and study drama. When he realised that he wasn't just going to be 'discovered' and had to put a lot of hard work into it with very little chance of becoming the star he dreamt of being, he soon changed his ideas. He is 15 now and wants to be a DJ, so here we go again!"

It is very easy to get into the habit of saying No to your teen; after all, here you are with a few decades of life experience under your belt so you expect to know better than your little upstart – why shouldn't you say No when you think it's appropriate? Well, the reason is that it is bad for their self-esteem because it implies that their judgment is in some way flawed and that they are not capable of knowing what's good for them (yes, yes, we know that this is true, but that is not the point). One way of dealing with such situations is to add a reason for the No; another good tip is to ask them what they would say if they were the parent (but beware, this technique could backfire). Another way is to bite your tongue and let them make their own mistakes, where it's safe to do so.

Allowing them independence in order to bolster their self-esteem is a tricky area because it is fraught with issues of personal safety and parental responsibility. However, there are ways to foster independence without compromising these concerns. Independence is not just about letting them make their own way to their mate's and back; it is about allowing them to make their own decisions, to have their own opinions and to recognise their own rights. It is about making them less reliant on you for approval and encouraging them to have their own mind. Doing this in the issues that are less important will give you greater strength when it really matters.

A final way to boost their self-esteem is to make sure that you really listen to what they have to say, show an interest in their lives and actively demonstrate your support for any lifestyle choices they make. This means resisting the urge to multitask – how many of us stack the dishwasher or perform some other menial task whilst our teen is trying to tell us something they consider important? It may seem like trivial chatter to you as you concentrate on the task in hand, but they may slip in something significant that is easy to miss. Stopping your chores will demonstrate that you are really listening and do consider what they are saying as worthy of your attention.

Other influences on your child's developing mind

So far, we have discussed your influence on your child's sense of self, but parents are certainly not the only, or indeed even necessarily the major, influence on their lives (see *Our survey said* later in the chapter). Others include school, friends, the media, pop stars, celebrities, computer games ... and even Big Brother housemates. School and peer pressure will be returned to in later chapters. For now, let us explore the role of celebrity on the teenage psyche.

Why are stars and celebs so important to teenagers? There are a number of possible explanations for today's teenagers' obsession with celebrity. These include:

The need for a role model. Young people, who are still developing their own unique self-identity, are often unsure about what sort of person they should be. Should they be outgoing or more reserved? Should they be sneering and cynical or upbeat and enthusiastic? Should they be a fashion victim or develop their own style? Having someone as a role model allows the uncertain teen to copy someone whom they think has got it right.

First crush. Many young people have their first 'relationship' with a celebrity. Of course, this is not a genuine relationship, but serves as an opportunity to try out the emotions that they will later need for real relationships. The feelings that they experience, the infatuation they have, the qualities they crave – all these are like a trial run for the real thing that, they hope, will hit later on.

"My daughter had an enormous crush on a footballer. I wrote to the team manager and asked for an autograph and received a signed photo which was stuck to the bedhead and kissed each night until his engagement was announced in the local paper. Fortunately she had moved on by then and was relieved that she could stop the ritual without losing face or upsetting me!" *Parent of teenage girl*

Crushes or obsessions with celebrities are perfectly normal and natural and should be dealt with sensitively. So try not to ridicule the object of their desire, even if you are secretly convinced that their idol is the last person on earth any sane individual would want to touch, never mind have a relationship with. A crush only becomes a problem if it starts affecting their schoolwork or grades or they begin to mimic undesirable behaviour. If this happens, you could try gently diverting their attention and energies in other directions such as hobbies and club memberships.

Lifestyle aspiration. Stars, for many teenagers, offer a glimpse of a world that they can only dream of. A world where they are the centre of attention, where they are admired and wor-shipped and have all the possessions that a teen could desire. So it may not be the person they admire so much as the lifestyle they aspire to.

Escapism. The demands of school, homework, exams and chores can create in even the most conscientious child the desire to escape – if only for the duration of the bus journey to school. Fantasising about their chosen celeb can provide a respite from their day-to-day concerns. So preoccupation with the current big-screen heartthrob can provide a useful purpose in allowing some downtime from real life.

The need to belong to a group. If all their mates are drooling after the latest pop sensation, your teen won't want to be left out. Young people have a strong need to belong because it boosts their self and social identity. Being a member of a group, whether it be supporters of a football team, a class at school or the local scout or guide troop, provides social identi-fication and validation; this simply means that being a mem-ber of a group offers a strong sense of belonging which is one of the things that teenagers need to feel good about them-selves. Social validation allows teens to check their beliefs and values against those of other group members.

Our survey said...

We asked parents how much positive or good influence they think their teenagers receive from a variety of sources. The most popular source of positive influence comes from parents themselves (not too surprising!) with 42% of parents saying that they provide 'a lot' of positive influences on their child. Next, more surprisingly perhaps, was the friends of the teenagers at 37%; this is despite all the parental worries about peer pressure. Much lower on the list were school and teachers (19%) and the internet (16%). Television was only thought by 7% of parents to offer a strong positive influence, with magazines (3%) and celebrities (2.5%) at the bottom of the list of good influences.

The importance of hobbies and interests

Exploring a number of hobbies and interests is a valuable part of your teen's development and you should probably encourage them if they show enthusiasm. There are many benefits to your child having hobbies:

- **Meeting people.** Going to clubs, after-school activities or interest groups provides a great opportunity to meet like-minded people and increase their circle of friends. This can be especially useful if they either don't have very many friends (e.g. if you've moved to a new area), or if, in your opinion, they have the 'wrong' kind of friends.

- **Relaxation.** Outside interests provide downtime from the pressures of school work. Sports and physical exercise allow the burning off of excess energy and have the added benefit of 'healthy body, healthy mind'.

- **Self-esteem.** Often, teens will gravitate towards an interest that they are good at, like football, chess or art; spending time doing something they are good at is likely to make them feel good about themselves. But even if they don't excel in their chosen pastime, they can still benefit from a shot of much-needed self-esteem simply by doing something that they enjoy and in which they can cultivate an interest.

- **Self-identity.** Adults tend to be labelled by their profession; the first question we ask someone we've just met is "What do you do?" The job title then, to some extent, defines your view of the person. Children, obviously, don't have this label, so hobbies and interests can provide an equivalent self-descriptor. Telling people that that you are in the swimming squad immediately conjures up a certain image which may be different from that conjured up by saying you are a member of the school chess club. This image, to others and yourself, contributes to your self-identity, or view of yourself.

- **Group identity.** Humans are naturally social animals and joining clubs satisfies our need to affiliate. It also has the added advantage of making sure we surround ourselves with like-minded individuals as this ensures that we feel more secure about ourselves.

As parents you should be aware that teenagers can pursue hobbies for wrong reasons as well as for the above good ones. Some children may feel pressured to pursue a hobby to please their parents; the need for approval can be very strong in this age group. You can put pressure on your children without even realising it; for example, having invested financially in their chosen interest, you may put pressure on them to continue even though they feel they have outgrown their hobby. Alternatively, it could be that the fact that you excelled at something thus putting implicit pressure on them to try to excel too. Or possibly, they know that you never had the chance to indulge in a particular hobby but your child knows you are desperate that they should make the most of the chance you never had.

A MOTHER'S STORY

"I always wanted to do ballet as a child but my parents couldn't afford the outfit or the fees. When I had a girl, I was determined that she would get the chance that I never had. On her third birthday, I enrolled her in the local ballet school, complete with pink tutu, ballet shoes, wrapover cardigan etc. By the time she was 12 she refused to go any more and I was devastated. She confided that she had only kept going the past few years because she knew how much it mattered to me."

Another potentially bad reason for pursuing a hobby is when it is due to peer pressure; doing something just because all their friends are doing it may lead to confused self-identity. They may think that they ought to enjoy the interest just because their friends do and this can create internal conflict, so encourage them to do things that they enjoy not that other people do.

Coping with your child's hobbies

One question you might find yourself asking is when encouraging your teen in their hobby becomes undue pressure. A good indicator that there may be a problem is if your teenager seems reluctant to go to the activity, practise it, or even talk about it. If you find yourself having to nag or cajole them, then you should take a step back as you may have crossed the fine line between encouragement and pressure.

"A mother I know was involved in her daughter's netball hobby, following the team everywhere, wearing the kit and generally interfering to promote her chances of being selected. The teenager dropped out. She then followed in the same manner to the next hobby, extolling her daughter's virtues at every opportunity and now wonders why her daughter stays in her bedroom in her spare time." *Parent of teenager*

Of course, it's easy to slip into nagging mode when you have spent half a month's salary kitting them out with football boots, shin pads, club strip and an England kit bag to carry it all in – only for them to decide after two weeks that they want to take up ballet à la Billy Elliot instead. Should you pile on the pressure and force them to do something they've lost interest in, or should you cut your losses and spend the other half of your salary on new ballet kit? Is it healthy for your teen to flit, butterfly-like, from hobby to hobby, or should you be encouraging them to develop 'stickability'?

There are advantages to both approaches: on the one hand this is the age when young people need to try out different activities so that they can find out what they like (or just as importantly, what they don't like) and what they're good at. This period of exploration contributes towards the development of their self-identity (as outlined above). On the other hand, teens need to be encouraged to develop a sense of commitment, especially if it is a team activity where they may be letting other people down. A practical solution might be to only allow them to take up a new hobby if they agree to commit for a reasonable amount of time, such as a term.

Finally, parents should be aware of the dangers of hothousing.

This is the term used to describe parents who rush children from activity to activity in a bid to expose them to as many valuable opportunities as possible. Teenagers, like adults, need time to relax, chill out and do nothing, so try to make sure that they have enough unstructured time.

This chapter has started to look at what makes your child who they are. The following chapter continues the theme of understanding your teenager by discussing how you can help your child to become their own person.

Chapter 2

Helping your teen become their own person

During the transition from childhood to teenhood, your precious ray of sunshine will evolve from being somebody happy to be like you and following your ideals and values, to a creature that makes every effort to separate themselves from you and all that you stand for. No longer will they share your tastes in clothes, entertainment and general activities – in fact it will seem as though they are opposing everything you suggest simply because it is your suggestion. In other words, they are becoming their own person, and don't you know about it.

Of course, an important part of child-rearing is helping them become their own person and this chapter is not about trying to stop this natural process. Rather it is about helping you cope with this difficult transition. It is also about helping your child become their own person and not the person their friends might want them to become – resisting that all-important peer pressure. And, of course, it's about you resisting the temptation to prolong that delightfully flattering 'mini-me' stage that characterises earlier childhood.

The first place to start then is with those all-important friends. After all, you don't want to swap a 'mini-me' for a 'mini-them'.

Friends and their influence

"I feel their friends influence them enormously at this stage – they are fiercely important to them." Parent of 16 year old girl.

"I would say that my daughter's friends are the biggest negative influence on her. Two have just had babies." Parent of 15 year old girl

"My daughter dare not be out of touch with her friends, she is constantly texting them to see what they are doing or who has said what and so on." Parent of teenage girl

Friends are central to your teen. Our research suggests that the whole issue of friends, friendship, fitting in etc is one of the biggest areas of concern for teenagers, with a third of parents we asked saying this was what their teens worried about most. Adolescence is the time when your teen begins to form meaningful and enduring friendships. Pre-teens need friends too but these tend to be playmates more than anything else. Children need friends to play with their dolls or cars, to act out scenarios in playgrounds and to play games with. As they mature into teenhood, deeper elements of friendship become more important, for example, providing someone to turn to for emotional support, loyalty and help with problems and worries.

As parents you will worry yourself silly about their friends and their influence over your teen. It may be hard for you to suddenly realise that their friends and their opinions seem more important to them than you. You will worry that their friends are not 'suitable', that they are having a bad influence and that they are undermining all the good groundwork that you have laid down in the last decade. These are not groundless worries as their friends may influence them more than you can. However, if you have built up their self-esteem and self-confidence, instilled good values and taught them to be assertive (see later section), you should feel as confident as you can be that your teen has the tools with which to defend themselves against malevolent influences. And don't forget that friends can have positive influences too – more than a third of our survey respondents thought that friends offered their teenagers 'a lot' of positive influence.

Understanding the power of peer pressure

"My 16 year old son is currently serving a three-month custodial sentence for assault and peer pressure played a big part in this." *Parent of teenager.*

"Her friends are her main influence – especially where alcohol and parties are concerned!" *Parent of 15 year old girl.*

"Her friends are the most important people in her life." *Parent of 14 year old girl*

"Our daughter and the other girls are like clones. They all dress and look the same. No one has an individual bone in their body." *Parent of 14 year old girl*

Teenagers care desperately about what their friends think. Their friends provide a social barometer against which they can measure their own behaviour, values, abilities and qualities. If they want to know how good they are at chemistry, they wouldn't necessarily compare themselves with their chemistry teacher, but might make the comparison with their peers. Similarly, if they want to know how funny they are, they would be more likely to value the laughs they got from their mates than those they got from their parents.

Comparing favourably to their peer group is of utmost importance to most teens, because they have the need to be similar to like-minded others. If they believe that they are similar then this reassures them that they are doing things right. This can mean that friends have immense power over your child's appearance, choice of clothes, interests, attitudes and values. As teenagers get older and become more confident in how to behave and what is expected of them, they may depend less on peer approval (though plenty of adults have yet to reach this stage!).

The role of friends

According to Gottman & Parker (1987), friends are important to teenagers for the following reasons:

- Companionship – teenagers need friends of about the same age to share their interests, dreams, fears and just to generally hang out with.

- Stimulation – friends provide entertainment, excitement and fun.

- Physical support – sometimes teens need more tangible support, for example a friend to accompany to them to a doctor's appointment, to share their resources such as magazines or books, or even just someone to lend them clothes or makeup.

- Ego support – teens need peers who can boost their self-esteem at all those insecure moments, for example offering reassurance that they look good in their new jeans.

- Social comparison – in times of uncertainty, teens may look to their friends for the appropriate way to behave. For example a new classmate joins the school and your teen may look to their friends to see whether or not to accept them.

- Intimacy/affection – teens need to develop warm and close relationships with people other than their parents, and close friends fulfil this role. This usually involves some degree of self-disclosure, such as sharing secrets and feelings.

Peer pressure is what happens when teenagers are influenced by their friends to do something that they perhaps wouldn't normally have done. It is important to understand that there are many different reasons teenagers succumb to peer pressure. These include being afraid of rejection by others, not wanting to be made fun of, worrying about hurting a friend's feelings, wanting to give the impression that they're grown-up, wanting to be cool and just generally wanting to be liked and accepted.

While peer pressure can be beneficial in encouraging your teen to do the good stuff such as taking up a new interest or carrying out voluntary work, peer pressure can also be responsible for the bad stuff like smoking, taking drugs, playing truant and the like. The key to helping your child to resist negative peer pressure is to build up their self-belief and confidence (see page 32). Teenagers who are self-confident, who value themselves and who feel secure are far more likely to be able to resist peer pressure.

Inoculating your teen against the effects of peer pressure

The trick to helping your teen to resist peer pressure is to *prepare them in advance*. There are a number of techniques that teens inevitably use to exert their influence: by training your teen to spot these, you can, in effect, inoculate them against most peer pressure that they will face. Peer pressure relies on the following main techniques:

■ The most powerful technique that your teen will face is the 'I-won't-be-your-friend' ploy. This starts in infancy and becomes more subtle as they develop so that by the time they hit their teens it can take many forms, from direct threats to more veiled intimidation.

■ Another technique is through the use of spurious arguments. Their friends may try and persuade using illogical, false or otherwise unconvincing reasons. Key giveaway phrases that your teen should look out for include: "nobody will ever know", "just once won't harm you", "everyone else is doing it", "if you loved me you would", "if you were really my friend you would".

■ Using insults is another way to pile the pressure on. Common jibes include: "Don't be a baby", "Grow up", "You worry too much", "You're such a wimp".

The best way to deal with these tricks is, like an inoculation, to immunise them before they are exposed to the insidious bug that is peer pressure. Find a good opportunity to discuss peer pressure before they experience it first-hand.

Try to convince your teen not to worry about the 'I-won't-be-your-friend' ploy because these are often nothing more than empty threats – a bit of 'bluff-calling' is maybe all that is required. And if it's not an empty threat, then gently point out that perhaps these are not the kind of friends that they really want. If you can get them to arrive at this conclusion themselves, so much the better.

Encourage your teen to think critically rather than accept at face value the superficial arguments that might be presented to them. For instance, "Everybody's doing it" – this is a statement that cries out for verification. A simple "How do you know that?" could suck the wind out of their sails for a lot of the spurious arguments. Warn your teen that arguments based on emotional blackmail ("If you loved me you would") should trigger loud wailing klaxons in their head – anybody who ever says this cannot care for you as much as you thought they did.

And finally, make your teen aware that resorting to childish insults is a last desperate attempt to persuade when all else has failed. When their mates are forced to rely on insults they know they are not going to win you round with argument or reason. Their last feeble fling is to hurl a few insults in the hope of riling them into submission. When the insults fly, tell your teen to simply walk away – and permit themselves a smug grin as they know they have won.

Helping your teen become more assertive

An important way in which your teen can become their own person is by developing assertion skills. Being assertive is about standing up for themselves and what they believe in, respecting their rights and those of other people (including yours), and expressing their opinions, desires and needs in a way that does not impinge upon those of other people. You should not be afraid of your teen becoming more assertive: some parents think that passive, malleable offspring are easier to manage and control. And indeed they are. But if they are easy to control by you, then they are just as likely to be easily controlled by the drug-taking, school-truanting, Asbo-seeking youths who hang out on every street corner. Teaching them to be more assertive may indeed mean they may stand up to you, but they will also be more likely to stand up to the 'horror' down the road.

Ask your teen to complete the following quiz, or perhaps answer the questions on the basis of how you think your teen would behave.

Please indicate how difficult you find the following things to do. Use the following scale:

1 = I think I could do this very easily
2 = I think I could do this quite easily
3 = I think this would be quite hard for me to do
4 = I think this would be very hard for me to do

☐ Turn down a request to borrow your iPod (or similar)

☐ Say something nice to a friend

☐ Ask a favour of someone (e.g. ask someone to get you a book from the library)

☐ Say sorry when you have done something wrong/made a mistake

☐ Turn down a request to go out with someone (date or friendship)

☐ Tell a family member if they do something that bothers you

☐ Admit to mates that you don't know something

☐ Admit in class that you don't know something

☐ Turn down a request to borrow money

☐ Try to 'shut up' a talkative friend

☐ Request a meeting or date with someone

☐ If your initial request for a meeting is turned down, ask again another day

☐ Admit to friends that you do not understand something

☐ Ask whether you have upset someone

☐ Tell someone you like them

☐ Complain about a faulty product or poor service

☐ Tell a teacher that you don't understand something

☐ Express an opinion or view that is different from your friends

☐ Tell someone that you think they are treating you unfairly

☐ Tell someone some good news about yourself

☐ Resist pressure from friends to do something you don't want to (e.g. drink alcohol, smoke etc)

☐ Ask for borrowed items to be returned to you

☐ Carry on talking to someone who disagrees with you

☐ Tell a friend that something they are doing bothers you

☐ Ask a person who is bothering you in public to stop

☐ Receive compliments

☐ Tell a teacher that you think they are treating you unfairly

☐ Ask an adult who is smoking close to you to stop

How to score: If they've scored mainly 1s and 2s, their assertiveness skills seem quite good. If they've scored mainly 3s and 4s, then their assertiveness skill are probably lacking – like most teens.

The first thing your teen needs to understand is the difference between assertion, passivity and aggression. Sometimes, teens become aggressive because they don't know any other ways to express themselves. Alternatively, they may be afraid to stand up for themselves because they are not sure whether they have the right to do so. The following two-stage process can be used to help your teen develop their assertiveness skills.

Stage one

A good starting strategy is to sit down with your teen and help them understand what their rights as a teenager actually are. The list below will help, but simply telling them the list is less effective than helping them generate some of the items themselves. You could do this by asking your teen to explain to you what their rights are, for example, in terms of their freedom, privacy, and treatment by other people.

Sample list of rights

- We all have a right to assert our needs, wants and feelings with other people: this means that we have the right to tell people how we feel.

- The right to ask for what we want – whilst remembering that other people have the right to say No.

- The right to have an opinion: but we should respect other people's rights to hold different opinions.

- The right to make our own decisions (but live with the consequences).

- The right to choose whether or not to get involved in the problems of someone else – and other people have the right to choose whether or not to get involved in our problems.

- The right to make mistakes – without lifelong recriminations.

- The right to change our mind: but we don't have the right necessarily to expect other people to like it.

- The right to a degree of privacy – and other people have the right to expect it from us.

- The right to be happy – but not necessarily at someone else's expense.

- The right to change ourselves – but not necessarily to expect other people to be happy with us changing.

- The right to make our own choices – even if these turn out to be the wrong ones.

- The right to say No if you feel that it's the right thing to do.

- The right to be treated with respect – and other people have the right to be treated with respect by you.

It is only by becoming aware of their rights that teenagers can know if these rights are being violated. For example, how can they say No if they don't really accept that they have the right to do so? How can they be expected to stand up to their friend if they don't recognise that they have as much right to happiness as them?

Stage two

The crux of being assertive is learning to say No. We all go through life being expected to do things that we don't want to do, but, for teens, those things could be illegal, harmful or just downright dangerous. Saying No is sometimes easier said than done, as any parent who agrees to run their school fête single-handed each year, or who finds themselves volunteered for that unpopular project at work, will testify.

Practise the following techniques with your teen and you may find that you both improve your ability to say No.

The Broken Record technique. This is where you simply repeat the No over and over again, perhaps in a slightly varying format. For example:

Friend: "Will you miss the last lesson and come shopping with me to buy a birthday present for my mate?"

Teen: "No, it's Geography and I don't want to miss it."

Friend: "Oh don't be so boring."

Teen: "I don't want to miss Geography."

Friend: "But you hate Geography."

Teen: "I still don't want to miss it."

Friend: "But you would if you were a real friend."

Teen: "I am your friend but I don't want to miss school."

And so on …

Reflecting. This is where you agree with the ideas expressed but still stick to your guns with the No. For example:

Friend: "Hey, do you want to come over to mine after school?"

Teen: "Sorry, no can do."

Friend: "But I was hoping we'd finish off our designs for the party invites."

Teen: "That would have been good but I can't."

Friend: "But I was really hoping to get them finished today."

Teen: "I realise that you would like to get them out of the way today but I can't come."

Reasoned No. This differs from the 'broken record' in that you give reasons for your refusal. This is a very powerful technique but it may be difficult for some teens to use because it requires a good line of arguments up your sleeve, and the ability to produce counter-arguments. For example:

Friend: "Can I borrow your mobile phone just for the afternoon."

Teen: "No, I'd rather not."

Friend: "But I've left mine at home and I need to text my boyfriend."

Teen: "No, because I don't like to go anywhere without my mobile phone."

Friend: "I'll give it to you back straight after Maths."

Teen: "No, I have only got a bit of battery power left and I need that for emergencies, and my account is running low."

Friend: "I'll pay you back for the texts."

Teen: "No, I need to make sure I have battery power for my journey home."

There are many resources and books about Assertion Training; the above is just a taster to get you started. Of course, none of this chapter is much use if your teen is reluctant to even talk to you (and, let's face it, many teens would rather have root canal treatment) so the next chapter looks at improving communication skills with your oh-so-monosyllabic teen.

Chapter 3

How to talk when they only grunt

"We try to talk to him but he finds it difficult to respond – this is very frustrating." *Parent of 17 year old boy*

"I am lucky to get a grunt if I ask her anything." *Parent of 13 year old girl*

"It is very hard to communicate with her as she just tells us to shut up." *Parent of 16 year old girl*

"Jade doesn't do 'conversation' with us." *Parent of 16 year old girl*

"I am kept in the dark. Anything she tells me is on a strictly need to know basis – and usually after the event." *Parent of 15 year old girl*

"Trying to establish a dialogue with a teenager can leave you emotionally battered and bruised. It is almost impossible to communicate with the monosyllabic teenager who actually doesn't want to speak and who regards you as brainless. Mark Twain describes it brilliantly: 'It is a very curious thing. When I was about 13 my father's intelligence started to drop. His mental abilities continued to decline until I reached 21 when these abilities began miraculously to improve.'" *Kindly supplied by Parent of a teenager*

"It can be very frustrating and hurtful when your teenager talks to you as if you were dirt under their fingernails and then you hear that same teenager talking in a very caring and 'normal' tone of voice to their friends." Parent of teenage girl

Effective communication can sometimes be a damnably difficult proposition, even with other allegedly rational adults. So be under no illusion that, when conversing with the skinful of raging and rebellious hormones that is your tetchy teen, your task is going to be a challenging one. And let's face it, you have a number of tricky topics that you will need to broach – from sex to smoking, from homework and money matters to future careers, chores and drugs, to name but a few of the more contentious ones. It makes you want to hide in a box and not come out until they have left home.

However, communicate with your teenager you must, even though at times this undertaking may well be a task of Herculean proportions that you have no wish to attempt: but without a firm line of communication between you and your teen, the battle is truly lost. Yet do not despair, this chapter will aid you in your mission and will guide you safely along the treacherous path that is talking to your teen. By drawing from the psychological literature on communication and language, clear signposts will be planted along the way to allow you to establish, and maintain, a full and fruitful dialogue with your offspring, despite the potentially tricky nature of some of the topics you will be required to tackle.

Our survey said...

How much do teens really communicate with their par-

ents? Is the grunting teenager a myth? Regrettably, our research suggests that the non-communicative teenager is only too real with parents complaining that their teens tell them little or nothing about the following areas of their lives:

- 28% of teens tell their parents little or nothing about their hobbies or interests

- 36% of teens tell their parents little or nothing about their friends

- 37% of teens tell their parents little or nothing about their hopes and dreams

- 38% of teens tell their parents little or nothing about school

- 45% of teens tell their parents little or nothing about their worries or problems

- 74% of teens tell their parents little or nothing about their boyfriends/girlfriends

In general, girls are a more communicative lot than boys. For example, 34% of girls tell their parents 'a lot' about school compared with only 20% of boys; 29% of girls tell their parents 'a lot' about their friends compared with only 9% of boys.

More than one way to skin a rabbit?

Many philosophers and poets have waxed lyrical about the importance of words in our communications with others. It was Confucius who said that "Words are the voice of the heart", whilst another wise soul claimed that "Words can make a deeper scar than silence can heal". However, if you ask a psychologist about the importance of words in communication you will get an entirely different view.

According to one eminent researcher, the contribution of words to the overall impact of our message is only 7%: the way we speak our message (for example, a high-pitched indignant tone or a staccato-style of speaking) contributes a further 38% to its overall impact. But by far the most important component of our message is that of our non-verbal behaviour (for example our crossed-arm, leaning-back posture and our wizard-like hand-waving) which contributes a massive 55% to the impact of our message. While other researchers question the exact levels that each individual factor contributes, all are agreed that what we say is not necessarily the important factor in our communication with others.

Therefore, you need to be careful to send out the desired message with your body language when communicating with your teen. Most of the time, our body language signals come naturally and the person that we're speaking to is in no doubt as to attitudes and feelings – when we're angry with our teen, our arm waving and raised voice leave them in no doubt that they crossed one of the many lines that they're not supposed to. However, there will be times when you need to disguise your body language to ensure that you are able to get your message across to your errant teen. Imagine the situation: your teen has come home two hours late on a Friday night, you've been worried sick and you just want to pick them up and throttle them and hug them in equal measure. However, if you want to explain to them that they have done wrong, ranting at them is not the most effective way.

Where possible, be aware of the following aspects of your non-verbal communication and try to keep them under control despite how you might be feeling at the time:

■ **Body posture**. Avoid crossing your arms, even though it might be a comfortable posture. It sets up a barrier between you and your teen, and they will pick up on this defensive posture.

■ **Hand gestures.** Try to keep your hands under control. Avoid pointing in an accusatory manner, though cutting out all hand gestures is not necessarily the best idea.

■ **Eye contact.** Try to keep your eye contact steady and avoid looking away from your teen – especially when you are feeling disappointed with them. Equally make sure you don't get into a staring contest with them as this may force your teen to look away and thus dilute the impact and content of your message.

■ **Distance.** You might find yourself moving closer and closer to your teen if you're angry with them, as you try to ensure that your message hits home. This may have the effect of encroaching on your teen's personal space, which at best will make them feel very uncomfortable (which may be your intention, but again it will detract from the impact of your message as they are more concerned with your closeness than what you are saying) and at worst will have them backing away from your approaching menace resulting in a bizarre dance around the room. At the same time, you don't want to put too much distance between yourself and your teen as this may send the subconscious message that you no longer love them – and whilst you might feel this at the time, there will be many more pleasant times in the future which you will not want to damage by one incident. Try to ensure the distance between you and your teen is the same as it is when you talk to them on a daily basis.

The box below gives further advice on using non-verbal communication in particularly sensitive communications with your teen.

Using non-verbal communication

It is essential that when dealing with some rather emotive topics that you do your best to put your teen at ease. There is perhaps nothing more uncomfortable than talking to your teenager about the basics of sex (see *Our survey said* in Chapter 7 about how uncomfortable parents are when talking about this). You may feel that it is your duty to tackle this thorny issue, but at the same time you may also be terribly embarrassed by the topic. And, mark our words, if you come across as being embarrassed, your teen will quickly pick up on this and one of two things will happen: if they are of a shy, retiring disposition, they too will become embarrassed and your chat will spiral downwards into a whirlpool of discomfort and non-communication, but if you're really unlucky, and they are a bit more streetwise than you give them credit for, they will rib you mercilessly for ever more about the day dad/mum tried to "give me the talk!" This is the point at which you are glad that you learned how to control your non-verbal behaviour.

The first thing to remember is to take a deep breath before starting to speak. Failure to do this will result in your voice being less than measured, and you may even start off with a squeak rather than the authoritative tenor you desired. Eye contact should be steady, but not too intense. Try not to appear as if you are plumbing the depths of their soul to discover their deepest, most sordid secrets. Also avoid looking away all the time as this will comprehensively send the message that you are embarrassed about your subject matter.

Even evidencing mastery of these three or four basic cues will alter the fundamental nature of your conversation. It will put you firmly in control of the situation and will avoid sending out negative messages about your feelings regarding the topic. It is also likely that your relaxed and open posture will be mirrored by your teen, as is the way with most conversational partners, and will create an atmosphere in which they should feel comfortable to tackle the topic.

Whilst non-verbal gestures are important in getting your message across, the words you use are also worth considering. If you know that you will be tackling your teen on a sensitive issue, it might be worth practising your delivery and thinking about the words that you might use. In any message, research tells us that we will remember the beginning and the end more than what goes in the middle – by having a well-rehearsed opening to your communication, you will give the best possible chance for the rest of your message to be taken on board. This will also ensure that you don't stutter and stumble over what you are trying to say, especially if your topic is slightly embarrassing or emotive, which may deflect your teen's attention away from the content of what you are trying to say.

When thinking about the words you are going to use, you might like to consider the outcome of a nifty psychological experiment that was carried out some years ago, which was based on the concept of psychological reactance – more commonly (and perhaps a little incorrectly) referred to as reverse psychology. Researchers tackled the problem of graffiti appearing on walls in public places by using two methods. In the first they displayed signs saying something like "Do not write graffiti on this wall as it is prohibited", and in the second they used wording along the lines of "Please refrain from writing graffiti on this wall". The results suggest that whilst the graffiti didn't disappear completely (miracles take slightly longer to work), it was significantly reduced when the second set of wording was used – the take-home message being that if you tell someone they can't do something, thus threatening their personal freedom, they're more likely to do it (and hence the concept of reverse psychology). Therefore, when you're talking to your teen, you might get better results by avoiding using categorical terms such as telling them that they cannot do something: so instead of saying, "You must not smoke cigarettes", you might want to try phrasing such as, "Your father and I would prefer you not to smoke".

You can reinforce the message by the use of *emotion and evidence*. In the first case, by making it clear to your teen that their behaviour is upsetting you, you are giving them a choice between upsetting you and not upsetting you. Now, while most teens will push the boundary and risk doing it once, in the long run by combining the two techniques, you may have more successful outcomes. Extending the above example to incorporate emotion will produce a message such as, "Your father and I would like you not to smoke as it upsets us". Expressing your feelings and needs directly is the best way to let your child know how their behaviour is affecting you.

The message can be further reinforced by bringing in factual evidence, whether you're talking about the dangers of smoking, unprotected sex or drug use. Information about the dangers of such behaviour is freely available on the internet (see later chapters for more resources) and by judicious research before such a conversation takes place you can strengthen the message you're trying to get across to your teen. Therefore, continuing the theme, you might open your communication with your teen regarding the dangers of smoking along the lines of: "Your father and I would like you not to smoke as it upsets us that you are putting your health at such risk. We've looked in to it and apparently figures suggest that your chances of developing lung cancer are multiplied by a factor of ten to twenty. We realise that it is your life to lead, but we're just worried about you." If you then ask your teen how they feel about this, you are likely to be on your way to effective communication. Don't be afraid to ask them to research the issues (via whatever medium they feel comfortable with – probably the internet these days) and ask them to let you know if they disagree with your findings.

And talking of disagreements, it is more than likely that your teen will not agree with most of your decisions. How you deal with these disagreements may be a major factor in determining the long-term quality of your communications with your teen. Don't be afraid to get them into the habit of thinking critically about issues. In this instance, if you give your reasons for a decision (such as a time for their weekday curfew), inviting them to weigh the pros and cons of your decisions, and inviting them to give valid arguments against your decisions will give your teen the feeling that they are involved in the decisions concerning them.

Quite clearly then, there are many ways to facilitate face-to-face communication with your teen, though clearly some of the methods outlined in this chapter will be more suited for older teens as opposed to the younger ones. Of course, you should always be looking to add to your armoury of communicative weaponry.

Another perhaps more subtle method of message delivery is the use of your own behaviour – sometimes, as they say, actions can speak far louder than words. In fact actions sometimes deliver a yodel of ear-splitting proportions from the mountain tops. For instance, if you smoke yourself, you may well find your message to your teen to stop smoking might fall on deaf ears no matter how dramatic and moving your rhetoric (though sometimes in these instances, it is our teens who are piling on the pressure to quit).

You also need to be aware that each of these weapons of mass communication is better suited for some situations over others – after all, when talking to your teen about the importance of becoming independent and starting to support themselves financially, you wouldn't necessarily want to go out and get yourself a paper-round to illustrate your point, or, when talking about the birds and the bees . . ! In these instances, words will do just nicely. And if this little cache of weaponry is not enough, let's throw another ingredient into your communicative cauldron – the use of environment. For everything there is a time and a place.

Use of the environment: framing your communication

Unless you choose the exact time and place to speak with your teen, you will find that your carefully chosen words and delivery will lose their impact. The delivery of your diatribe may be worthy of the Royal Shakespeare Company itself, but if your teen is ensconced in front of the box engrossed in either United's titanic struggle against City or the antics of the latest Big Brother evictee, your pleas or pearls of wisdom will indeed fall on the proverbial deaf ears.

Make sure also that your location is a neutral one (perhaps the kitchen), or perhaps, if you're feeling particularly plucky, even tackle them on their home ground (such as the pit from which they drag themselves each morn). If at all possible, try to avoid value-laden venues, such as the family study (with mum and dad's university or college certificates hanging on the wall) for a discussion on your teen's school grades, or your master bedroom for a casual tête-à-tête about sex. Such venues tend to act as barriers to open dialogue and will merely serve to put your teen on the defensive, anxious to be gone from the room at the earliest possible opportunity and with all possible haste.

You should also be careful to ensure that the venue will be free from interruptions, such as from siblings, relatives, insurance salesmen and other unwanted visitors. There will be nothing worse than, having struck the correct level of gravitas to tackle your teen's failing school grades, to have Mr Floppy, the beloved family cat, pad furtively into the room and comically flop into your lap at the pivotal moment of your oration.

Timing is also of paramount importance. When planning what you are going to say to your teen, you need to consider how long you think it will take in order to allow plenty of time for discussion of the issues. If you estimate that it will take half-an-hour, then double it to ensure that you have plenty of spare time (we're notoriously bad at estimating timings). This will mean that, if you are planning a talk with your teen about the importance of them starting to earn their keep, you should probably avoid squeezing it in the break of Coronation Street or even at half-time of a football match that they are watching on TV. You should also be aware that you may need more than one talk about some more complex issues that you need to discuss.

You need to be flexible as to the timing of the talk, too. If you have prepared an hour in which to have a chat with your teen when they return from school, be aware of their mood. If you judge them not to be in a receptive mood and they show the indications of being irritable (are they ever not irritable?) after a particularly bad day in the classroom you should be prepared to postpone your communication until a better time, assuming that it can wait an extra day or two. Psychology tells us that we are more receptive to the content of a message when we are in a good mood, and your teen is no different.

As you can see, there are many factors to be considered when planning the delivery of your communication. Overall, the advice is to choose your weapons of mass communication with care, and your battleground with caution.

Of course, talking to your teen is only one side of being able to communicate with them. You should also be prepared to listen – two of the most popular lines delivered by a teen to their parents are probably "You never listen to me" and "You don't understand me". Listening is an under-rated skill and one that is quite tricky to master, but good listening skills lead to better understanding.

Lend me your ears ...

We all like to think that we're good listeners but we're probably not as good as we think we are. Research shows that we all have a limited attention span and we're soon distracted by other thoughts. Here are seven tips for effective listening:

1 Each time you have a conversation with your teen, try to learn something new about them. Over the years, this will become more and more tricky, meaning that you need to be listening carefully to what they say, and be prepared to pick up on things hidden away amongst their general ramblings. It can be a small thing, such as the mention of a new name from school that you've not heard them use before or more meaningful information such as their mention of a new hobby they might like to pursue.

2 Focus on what your teen is saying and don't let your own thoughts distract you from this. For instance, if your teen trundles in from school in a talkative mood, and you're in

the middle of a work assignment or balancing the household bills, it might be hard to focus on their words without being distracted by your own concerns. Equally your teen's ramblings might lead you to start reminiscing about your own teenage days, and before you know it, you're dominating the conversation with your own lovely anecdotes. While it is good to share, you need to be aware that your teen may have been building up to saying something important, so be careful not to hijack their conversation. Sometimes it is good just to let them talk.

3 Show that you've been listening, and there are two main ways of doing this – reflection and questioning. Reflection involves repeating back to your teen what they've just said, but in a slightly different way. For example if they've just been telling you about the latest outstanding footballing exploits of their friend James, you could show that you've been paying attention by saying something along the lines of "So James has been a bit active on the football field, huh? Sounds like he might have a career there …" Try to avoid overdoing it though – a summary at the end of their period of conversation will be just fine: don't feel the need to do it at the end of each sentence. Similarly, questioning shows that you've been listening. After all, it's not easy to ask a question if you haven't heard a word they've uttered. So asking whether your teen thinks James has a chance of becoming a professional footballer should do the trick. And don't be afraid to ask questions in order to get more information. For example, if you haven't understood a single word they've been saying despite giving them your undivided attention, it shows that you really do care – though don't always expect them to explain. However, be aware that at times questions can be a little intrusive, and you should resist the urge to know absolutely everything about your teenager, such as what they are thinking and planning. Show them some trust.

4 Don't try to give them advice unless asked for it. During periods of conversation, they might start talking about situations that they are encountering at school and which you encountered as a teenager. Don't immediately assume that this is your opportunity to intervene with some advice – it probably isn't and such advice may well be unwelcome. By all means ask some follow-up questions if you deem it to be appropriate (given the warning in Point 3), such as "How do you feel about that?" This will then give them the opportunity to ask for help, but if they don't then trust them enough to find the solution on their own.

5 Try to match the mood of your teen. If they've come home in a good mood and want to talk, but you've had a bad day, this may not be easy to do. However, good communication can be facilitated by reflecting the mood of your teen.

6 Aim for empathy, not sympathy. Simply put, when they are telling you about their problems (which if you've developed your listening skills well, they will eventually feel comfortable doing), avoid saying a rather bland, "Aww, poor you". Instead, try to put yourself in their shoes and imagine how they are currently feeling. This will usually lead you to say the right thing. Of course, actions sometimes speak louder than words, and a hug instead of saying anything can work just as well.

7 Try to think before you speak. Having listened to someone (on occasion, for a long period of time), it is natural for you to want to take your turn to speak. However, make sure you don't just start blurting out any old rubbish, especially if what your teen has been telling you has been traumatic or embarrassing. Instead, count to five and allow yourself time to think about what to say next.

Other barriers to communication

Despite having developed many tools that will lead to positive communication between you and your teen, there are still other barriers that you need to be aware of and avoid:

■ Avoid using 'put downs'. As infuriating as your teen will be at times, you need to keep your cool and avoid saying things that will be unhelpful. These include phrases such as "That is rubbish" and "You don't know what you're talking about". These may be true, but serve absolutely no purpose in keeping positive communication channels open between you and your teen.

■ Avoid ordering and prescribing. You may believe that the power in the relationship between you and your teen is firmly weighted in your favour – and this is undoubtedly the case. However, using language that reinforces this position can be quite counterproductive. For example, telling your son that he must clean his room or your daughter that she can't have an increase in her allowance simply "Because I said so" is not helpful. Where possible try to give a reason for any decision that you make. It may help your teen to understand your motivations and may eventually help them to understand where you are coming from.

Generally this chapter has been about communicating with your teen regarding major issues. However, be aware that in the day-to-day scheme of things, you should be always be looking to foster good conversation between you and your teen. Some ways to do this include:

- When talking to your teen, for example at mealtimes or while watching TV, try to choose different topics of conversations. It is easy to fall into the habit of talking about the same old things, such as their school performance, reminders of chores they need to do, plans for their future or family events. It might be nice from time to time, if you judge the atmosphere to be right, to get them to talk about their feelings, ideas or plans. If your teen seems particularly receptive, why not get them to choose a topic of conversation for once – it will give them a feeling of empowerment.

- Don't be afraid to praise your teen – they probably don't get enough of it. If you're talking about current affairs, for example, and they have an interesting take on things, don't forget to tell them when you think they have a good idea, or that you didn't realise that they were so well-informed about issues. It will give them added self-confidence (which, as pointed out in previous chapters, can only be a good thing).

- Be prepared to laugh when your teen makes a joke, rather than keep a straight face. This should be as natural as possible – so don't force it if what they say really isn't funny. This will increase their self-esteem and make them feel more comfortable conversing with you. Empathising in other ways, as mentioned previously, will have a similar impact and should be a cornerstone of how you communicate with your teen.

It is worth taking the time to master the general communication techniques outlined in this chapter as they will be essential in tackling the specific issues covered in future chapters.

Chapter 4

Tears and tantrums

Even the most optimistic parent will agree that some conflict with their teen is inevitable – whether it is about relatively minor issues such as the appalling health hazard that is their bedroom, or more major issues such as the unwelcome (for you) distraction presented by their latest boyfriend or girlfriend. This chapter will help you understand that such conflict is a normal part of teendom, which may not make you feel any better about it, but our tips on coping with your antsy teen will. Read on and wonder how you ever coped before.

Why conflict with teenagers is unavoidable – but healthy

Parental conflict comes naturally to a teen. The transition from cute and cuddly child to spotty, hormone-fuelled adolescent brings with it many challenges as your teenager wrestles with their changing sense of self. Conflict erupts for many reasons, including the following:

■ The need to exert independence. A normal part of growing up involves the transition from dependent child to independent adult, and your teen is caught somewhere in-between. They may at times yearn for independence, but at other times seek the security of being 'mummied'. The real problem is that their yearnings for independence probably don't coincide with when you feel such independence is appropriate. Similarly, when they revert back to childhood you may just be expecting them to grow up and act their age.

■ Resentment of the familiar. For the past decade or so, your child may have been content to join in the family rituals, such as Sunday lunch or visiting relatives – activities which suddenly now evoke bitter complaints. This is because now they have a need to experience new things and to expand their repertoire of all that life has to offer. Added to this is the fact that familiar rituals are associated in their fast-developing minds with their childhood and this is a cloak which they now wish to cast off.

■ The all-important need to push boundaries. Teenagers have an emerging sense of self-identity, they are becoming a distinct individual, separate from their parents – and they feel the need to reinforce this. One way in which they do this is to challenge the boundaries as set down by their parents. They are effectively saying, "I'm different from you, I'm my own person."

■ They want to show they're grown up. A lot of parental conflict comes from teens wanting to do things that their parents think are too grown-up for them. For a teen, being older is cool (until they get their first wrinkle) so the faster they can accelerate into adulthood the better. Doing 'grown-up' things makes them feel more important, that

they will be taken more seriously and get the freedom
they crave.

■ Their rebellious hormones. For a teen, their emotions just
won't behave. One minute they are weepy and sensitive,
the next they are aggressive and bolshie. The nuances
and complexities of emotions are an alien landscape for
teens, so they really cannot control them as well as adults
can (or are, at least, supposed to). For the pre-teen, emotional experiences are much more black and white, but
once the hormonal cocktail is released by the onset of
puberty, the picture becomes more confused. Feelings such
as jealousy, injustice and love become much more pro-
nounced once puberty grabs hold of them and turns the
world as they know it upside down. For more on puberty,
see Chapter 7.

■ Difficulties in communicating their needs. Good
communication is an acquired skill so it is not surprising
that teens may be lacking in this department. For example, negotiation skills, conflict resolution and assertiveness skills are only really gained through life's rich
experience (or some very expensive corporate training
courses). For more on communicating with your teen, see
Chapter 3.

■ Everything is a personal insult. Teenagers are very sensitive souls and are likely to read far too much into the
smallest innocuous event. For example, cook them a meal
they don't like and they take it as a sign that you do not
love them as much as their sibling, or refuse to extend
their curfew and they accuse you of not trusting them. It

can seem at times that they are just looking for excuses to pick a fight. One of the reasons they may do this is because they lack the experience of life necessary to put things in context and depersonalise apparent slights.

So these are the main reasons why conflict with your teen is inevitable, but before you bang your head in despair against the nearest brick wall, you may take some small sliver of comfort from the knowledge that many experts believe conflict to be healthy. It is thought that allowing teens the opportunity to practise their negotiation skills in a safe environment is beneficial. In early teenhood, conflict may be characterised by slamming doors and stamping feet (and your teen may not behave well either!), but it is likely that, towards the end of their teens, they become more sophisticated in their persuasion techniques (and you may well yearn for the return of the door-slamming days).

Another reason why conflict is healthy for teens (if not for you) is that it allows an outlet for all those pent-up teenage emotions that bubble threateningly, geyser-like, waiting to erupt. Experts argue that suppressing emotions is harmful for mental health, and contrary to some parents' beliefs, will not make them go away. It is far better to let them out in a controlled environment than for them to seek another outlet which may be far more destructive.

So, the next time your teen hurls abuse ballista-like at you for running out of their favourite cereal, reassure yourself that this is taking them one step nearer to becoming a real human being. You hope.

Common conflicts

Having talked about the reasons for conflict, identifying the most common causes of conflict is the next step. It is useful to do this because knowing what other parents row with their teens about can offer reassurance that your relationship with your teen is normal(ish).

What are the main sources of parental conflict with teenagers?

We asked 170 parents what their top three sources of conflict were. Here are the findings in order of popularity:

1 Untidiness/messy bedroom – 30% of respondents
2 Homework issues – 26%
3 Attitude/lack of respect – 24%
4 Time spent on computer/phone – 15%
5 Money/spending/demands for money – 12%
6 Doing chores – 10%
7 Personal hygiene – 9%
8 Fighting with siblings – 9%
9 Staying out too late – 8%
10 Not getting up on time/going to bed too late – 8%
11 TV (watching too much/too loud etc) – 8%
12 Diet (too much junk food/not eating enough) – 7%
13 Swearing/bad language – 6%

Other sources of conflict included not telling parents where they are going, bad temper, drugs/alcohol/smoking, playing loud music, not communicating enough with parents, and the friends teenagers keep.

Approaches for dealing with conflict

Test yourself – how do you cope with conflict with your teen?

Tick the sentences that apply

- It is important that my teen shows respect for me during an argument

- It is important for me to show I am right

- My teen is rarely right

- Arguments with my teen always end in a row

- I usually raise my voice when I disagree with my teen

- My teen usually storms out during an argument

- I always seem to be rowing with my teen

- It often feels like my teen is my enemy

- My teen often accuses me of not listening to them during an argument

- We often bring up past grievances during our arguments

The more of these statements you ticked, the more your conflict resolution skills need working on (and, actually, the more typical a parent you probably are). Below are some key strategies for dealing with conflict with your teen.

Strategy 1 Avoid 'negative effect reciprocity'

This rather grand term simply means that when your teen

starts throwing insults and accusations at you, resist the very human urge to give as good as you get. It is human instinct to defend yourself by attacking, but it is counterproductive with anyone, especially with your teen. Remember that your teen may be testing you (see the reasons above for why conflict occurs) so don't feed their insecurities by giving them a reason to doubt your love. It is hard to stand there and take it calmly on the chin, but if you are to resolve the conflict effectively, you may just have to bite the bullet and take it. This is a de-escalation technique (see below)

Strategy 2 Try to stay in 'adult' mode

Transactional analysis is an approach that assumes that we can take on one of three roles in any of our transactions or interactions. We can either be Adult, Parent or Child. Being a 'Child' means that you are acting like a child, for example being petulant, illogical and emotional and displaying other behaviours that you might expect of a five year old. Adults can easily slip into this role too. Your teen will probably be exhibiting 'Child' behaviour while desperately trying to be 'Adult'. Being an 'Adult' means that you are trying to maintain an equal relationship with your adversary, whereas being the 'Parent' is about demonstrating your superiority in terms of power and knowledge. Most teenage conflict revolves around the parent in 'Parent' mode and the teen in 'Child' mode, whereas successful outcomes are more likely if both you and your teen can become the 'Adult'.

But how do you turn your stroppy teen into an 'Adult'? The best way is for you to stay 'Adult'; once you go into 'Parent' mode it is very hard for your teen to move out of the responsive 'Child' mode. So how do you stay 'Adult'? You can do this by staying calm, avoiding 'negative effect reciprocity' (see above), not treating them like a child, avoid being patronising or condescending and looking for rational solutions rather than emotional point-scoring.

Strategy 3 Using de-escalation techniques

De-escalation techniques have the effect of smothering the fire rather than adding fuel to the flames. Arguments have a habit of escalating out of control as each party reciprocates with a louder tone, a stronger accusation or a more offensive insult. De-escalation techniques include apologising and agreeing. Both of these techniques tend to take the wind out of their sails: as they gear up for another onslaught, a quiet "I'm sorry" or "You're right" can stop them in their tracks.

Using this strategy does not mean that you have to capitulate to your teen; it simply allows you to calm the waters in preparation for more 'adult-to-adult' discussion. It is highly possible to find something that you can agree with or apologise for without conceding the main argument. For example, you could agree that you shouldn't have lost your temper or that you are sorry for shouting. Hopefully this will de-escalate the situation enough to allow for a more productive discussion.

Another de-escalation technique that will throw them is to do something odd or out of the ordinary. For example, suddenly grab a banana from the fruit bowl, use it as a microphone and yodel your favourite Sound of Music number. Or leaping, twinkle-toed, on the kitchen floor and giving it your best Fred Astaire/Ginger Rogers impression. Well, you get the idea.

Anything that is likely to get your teen to stop in their tracks (but not get you committed to the local asylum) and interrupt the anger cycle long enough to defuse the situation.

Strategy 4 Using humour

Humour should be used with great care. When employed effectively it can be a very powerful tool to defuse a potentially explosive situation. However, it can backfire and your teen may think you are trivialising something they care about. The trick is to use it sparingly (and *never* use sarcasm) and to do so by perhaps identifying something funny in the situation that will tickle you both. For example, this could be by stumbling over your words, referring to a TV moment, or a current family in-joke. Humour works by interrupting the anger-arousal system, giving valuable time-out in which calming down can be facilitated.

Strategy 5 Deflecting

This is a 'buying time' strategy designed to put some distance between you and your rage-fuelled teen, in the hope that at least one of you will have calmed down by the time you return to the topic of contention. One way of doing this is by saying that you agree that there is an issue here that needs to be tackled, and that you would like to think about it further before giving your response – and arrange a time to meet up again later.

Presenting a united front

Teens are not daft and learn pretty early on that 'divide and conquer' is a strategy that can work when all else fails. For the uninitiated, this is where (using the example of a two-parent family) mum says No so the conniving little scallywag totters off on their precociously high heels (the girls as well) to dad. Dad, of course, in the absence of context and knowledge of mum's decision (and with his favourite TV programme about to start) quickly acquiesces – and all hell breaks loose between mum and dad. You get the picture.

Of course, this can be even more exacerbated where you do not live together with an ex-partner or there are multiple parents due to separation, divorce and parents finding new partners. If you are a single parent, you will have issues of being the one who is seen as always saying No and will need to manage other individuals, such as grandparents or occasional partners, who your teen may look to play off against you. See Chapter 8 for more on family relationships.

So, how do you combat the 'divide and conquer' strategy? Either delay making a decision until you can confer with your other half, or, even better have a house rule that if your child asks one parent when they already have an answer from the other, they get an automatic No (and their pocket money docked for life). Where you do not live with another parent, communication between yourselves is vital to ensure that your teen does not keep playing you off against each other. It is imperative to set aside animosity you may feel for your ex-partner and be as united as possible when it comes to parenting decisions. Allowing your teen to believe they can get what they want in this way will, ultimately, be harmful for your relationship with them and their own social development. A person who believes they can get their own way by playing others off against each other will have problems in building trusting relationships in their adult life. It is much better for you to be seen as strict now so that your child will benefit in the longer term.

This is all well and good if you are in agreement with each other, but it is inevitable that you and your co-teen trainer will not always see eye-to-eye on important issues. Perhaps you are relaxed about the hours they keep but your partner wants them tucked up safely by 11pm on a school night; or maybe you don't want them going out 'dressed like that', but your partner thinks they look pretty cool and trendy. The best strategy for dealing with such situations is prevention rather than cure. Hopefully you will have found out where you each stand on important issues before they arise and will have agreed what stance to take.

Of course, this is in an ideal world, but it is just as likely that an issue will jump up and take you by surprise before you have a chance to even think about it. In this case, you need to give yourself time to consider it together and not make any hasty decisions (even though your impatient teen wants an answer *now*), and you need to do this without your teen present to witness the tears and tantrums that may well diminish you in their eyes (especially if you are partial to throwing plates).

Use of ground rules, behaviour contracts and other teen-management techniques

Whilst tears, tantrums and conflicts are inevitable when owning a teenager, there are some preventive techniques that you can use to reduce their likelihood. Just as organisations and businesses have clear behaviour management policies in place to limit staff deviance (such as smoking where they shouldn't, skiving too much, or stealing more than Post-its and paperclips), so an effective parent ought to have similar management strategies in place.

Just as at work, the foundation of a good disciplinary policy is to have *clear ground rules*. These may include:

- Curfew times (both weekday and weekend/school holidays).

- Consequences of breaking said curfew: these should be clearly specified and known by all parties.

- Behaviour in the house, such as leaving coffee cups to fester in the bedroom.

- Expected household chores.

- Reward systems, such as pocket money allowance.

- House guests – who, when, where and how many.

- Computer and television usage – when, how long etc.

- Homework/social life balance – what has to be done before they go out, watch television etc.

- Use of house phone and mobile – whether this is unlimited, restricted, who pays etc.

- Keeping you informed of their whereabouts – it is important that you are both clear as to when your teen is expected to 'check in' with you (and maybe even for you to check in with them).

- Use of the car – if appropriate.

- Borrowing stuff – whether they can help themselves to the contents of your wardrobe, loose change jar or CD collection (as if).

- Food – whether they can help themselves to stuff in the fridge/cupboard whenever they like.

Our survey said...

The most common means of disciplining their teens for parents in our research were:

- **Grounding them – 40.5%**
- **Restricting use of computer – 40%**
- **Stopping pocket money/allowance – 29%**
- **Stopping treats – 28%**
- **Restricting TV use – 23%**
- **Giving more chores – 17%**
- **Restricting use of mobile phone – 16%**
- **Restricting use of family landline – 12%**

There may be other rules you need, but you get the gist. The main thing is that whatever ground rules you have should be strictly and consistently enforced. If you don't do this, your teen will quickly sniff out your weak spots and, before you know it, your ground rules will have been rapidly eroded.

Another good general teen-management strategy is that of the **behaviour contract**. This turns the ground rules into more of a two-way street, as you each agree the behaviour that is expected. In the workplace, this is similar to your job contract, whereby you agree to behave in a particular way in return for the expectation that your employer treats you in an appropriate manner. For you and your teen it might simply be a case of you both agreeing to show respect and to listen to each other, to keep each informed of the other's whereabouts, to respect each other's space and privacy, and so on. For some, it may simply be a case of agreeing to the contract verbally, but for others it may need a signing ceremony equivalent to that of the Magna Carta at Runnymede.

Action plans are another good way of ensuring teen compliance. This is where you and your teen sit down and agree a framework of what is expected of your teen and when. This is particularly useful in cajoling your reluctant teen into an acceptable balance between homework, chores and that all-important social life. Many points of conflict originate from a clash between these three demands: your teen does not necessarily share your priorities. Writing a clear action plan when you're both feeling calm and rational can pre-empt those frequent flashpoints and head them off at the pass.

Calming techniques for you and them

Despite your best efforts (and the efforts of this book), there will be times when you're at the end of your tether, you'll be screaming at each other and you both have lost it. This is when a good selection of calming tactics is essential to have in your metaphorical toolbox of skills. The following are taken from *Anger Management in a Week* (Sandi Mann, Hodder & Stoughton).

- **Engage in behaviour that is incompatible with anger.** Anger is a state of arousal and it is impossible to experience this if you are relaxed. So, if you are able to engage in an activity that makes you feel relaxed, it will not be easy for you to feel anger at the same intensity. If possible, you could try walking away and going for a calming walk, swim or any other activity that you find relaxing, creative or artistic pursuits, looking after pets or anything that you generally find relaxing.

- **Do something distracting.** This is a technique aimed at distracting yourself from the anger stimulus and thus reducing the intensity of the anger response. Distraction techniques include both physical and mental techniques. Physical distractions include doing some physical activity that occupies your mind (it does not have to be a relaxing activity like in the above technique). So, you could turn your attention to a particular piece of work that requires your concentration, read an interesting newspaper article or go and talk to somebody about something completely different. Mental distraction techniques include things such as mentally planning a menu for a dinner party or working out a route to a meeting in another part of town. You may not be physically engaged in a distracting activity, but as long as your mind is distracted then this technique can work.

- **Use of thought-stopping.** This is another cognitive or

mental technique that involves you 'catching' the anger response processes and interrupting them. When you feel your anger rising you interrupt the anger response by telling yourself to 'stop' the thoughts from going around your head; when we are angry, we tend to go over and over in our heads what has happened which causes the anger cues to continually be reinforced. This might involve saying the word "Stop", "Enough" or "No to yourself". It could be visualising a Stop sign like you might see for cars on the roads. It could even be a physical sign such as pinching your hand or snapping a rubber band onto your hand. Such signs can be enough to stop the stimulus and interrupt the anger response.

Having shown you some general techniques for dealing with conflict with your teen, it is now time to look at some more specific situations that will test your parenting skills and patience. We start with their school days.

Chapter 5

School days – happiest days of their lives?

School, exams and coursework are a major preoccupation for teenagers and their parents – for fairly obvious reasons. School is where kids spend most of their lives and success or failure can affect their entire future. School and exams were almost the top worry for parents we surveyed, with 27% citing this as something they worry about (see Chapter 9). It was the top issue that they thought their teens worried about, with 40% of respondents naming school/exams/coursework as the thing their teens worry about most.

Meeting with teachers: when to do it, how and what to say

There's something about meeting with 'Miss' or 'Sir' that makes you feel as though you are back in a gymslip or school tie yourself. It is easy to feel intimidated or even defensive, but the following guidelines will help you get the most out of these meetings:

- Parents' evening meetings are usually very strict in terms of time allocation – it is not unusual to be allocated only five minutes to discuss your child's progress. This doesn't seem much (unless they get a good telling off, in which case it will seem like five hours) but they do have a lot of parents to get through so rationing like this is the only way. Try to stick to time – if you have any further issues, arrange a separate meeting outside of parents' evening.

■ Have questions planned in advance; there's nothing worse than walking away realising that you forgot to ask about their new role as litter monitor (see below).

■ Take pen and paper to make notes of comments and/or grades given. You should be able to discuss these with your child when you get back. Your teen won't thank you if you tell them that they are a genius at something but you can't quite remember what.

■ Listen and don't get too defensive over any criticisms. Try not to take them personally, especially if you get the impression that the teacher in question really doesn't like your darling teen. It happens sometimes.

■ Make sure you have read any report that has been sent home in advance of the meeting and made note of strengths and weaknesses to discuss with the teacher. You could also discuss each subject with your child to see if they have any issues that need raising.

Making the most of parents' evening

The Parents Centre, a government initiative, has a useful guide about making the most of parents' evening that can be found at **www.parentscentre.gov.uk/educationandlearning/ schoollife/getinvolved/pupilreportsandparentevenings/**

It recommends asking the following questions at parents' evening:

- What are my child's strengths?
- Has my child shown any special talents?
- What is my child finding difficult? How can I help with this?
- Does my child try hard enough?
- Does my child join in class discussions?
- How can I help with my child's schoolwork in general?
- Has my child made sufficient progress since his last report?
- Is my child happy at school?
- Has my child made friends?
- Does my child's behaviour give any cause for concern?

Choosing subjects and other academic decisions – how to help your teen make the right choices

Making the right choices is always an emotive subject for parents for a number of reasons:

- We think we know best.

- We think our kids are too immature to have a sensible long-term view.

- We think we know best.

- Up to now, we have probably made all the most important, life-changing decisions for our children – it is hard to relinquish control.

- We think we know best.

Of course, these are all perfectly true and valid; teens do find it difficult to see beyond the next year or so, we have made most of the important decisions to date (and they haven't turned out too badly, have they?) and, of course, we do know best. So, the temptation to direct, cajole or otherwise steer your stubborn teen into the career path of your choosing is great. But you must resist! That way lies, if not madness, then revolt, tantrums and rebellion (theirs, if not yours).

By the time children reach the stage of life-changing decisions at school, they are almost human and, as such, need to be empowered to make their own decisions. Foisting academic subjects on them, even if it's for their long-term benefit, will not be conducive to success. As the saying goes, you can lead a horse to water, but you can't make it buckle down and revise Latin prose. Teenagers, more than any other creatures, need to feel that they are making their own choices and steering their own path in life. Your job, as caring parent, is to help them make their own decisions and keep your mouth firmly sealed when they insist on leaving school to join the circus (and is that really so bad?).

Choices they might need to make include: what subjects to choose for GCSE or A Level, what university course to study, where to study, whether to leave school and get vocational training, whether to leave school and get a job, start their own business, take a gap year in Outer Mongolia, or even run off with their girlfriend/boyfriend, get married and be a parent. Trying to choose between various options is daunting for any teenager, so use these tips to help them (and you) cope:

■ Try not to be too judgemental. Sometimes kids say things

to try and shock you, so if you react furiously to their sudden announcement that they want to quit school to take up limbo dancing, your reaction may just be enough to make them dig their heels in. Best to be calm and they are less likely to experience 'psychological reactance' – whereby we want to do something just because we know we can't.

■ Sit down with them and go through their options in a systematic and rational way. Help them decide what they are good at and where their weaknesses lie (not just in academic subjects – bring in their Brownie experience, their Duke of Edinburgh's awards and their art prizes).

■ Discuss their aspirations and what is important to them; would they prefer a well-paid job or one that gave them job satisfaction? Would they prefer to study a subject they enjoyed or one that had the most career potential? Is being with their friends more important than choosing the best subject? All these questions will help steer the right path for them.

■ Narrow down the choices and weigh up the pros and cons for each option. Make a list for each choice and perhaps they could even give weightings for each pro and con.

■ Encourage your teen to visit the school careers or Connexions adviser or, if they may prefer to see someone out of school, your local Connexions office [**www.connexions-direct.com/whichwaynow**]. You may also find it useful to chat with them yourself as Connexions now base their advice on looking at your child in the round, including their family circumstances, rather than just at academic issues.

- Find out what qualifications they will need for their chosen career path (if they have one). The school careers or Connexions adviser should be able to help with this but also check out the Connexions website [**www.connexions-direct.com/jobs4u/**].

Coping with 'grade-dropping' and reluctance to study

What happens when your teen refuses to buckle down and study? Most kids prefer to go out with their mates, watch TV or kick a football around the garden than revise or do homework (and can we really blame them?), but some seem to resist studying more than others. Their grades start falling because they are simply not putting the hours in. It is natural for ambitious parents to be concerned and to get angry or upset, but it is important to take a step back and ask yourself (or better still, your teen) the following questions:

- Is my child happy at school?

- Is there some other reason that might account for the change in work ethic (such as family trauma, boyfriend/girlfriend troubles, bullying etc)?

- Does your child like their subject/form teacher?

- Is your child's behaviour different in other areas (e.g. do they seem depressed, angry, resentful – more than usual, that is)?

- Have their career aspirations changed?

- Do they have low 'academic self-esteem' (i.e. do they have little faith in their academic abilities)?

- Are they concerned about the expectations you (or others) might have of them?

Identifying the root cause of the problem is the first important step. There is no point grounding them, shouting at them or threatening them if they are deeply unhappy about something and it is this that is affecting their ability to study. You may have to dig a bit before they will open up; after all, if they expect you to fly off the handle, they will not be terribly forthcoming. You will need to build their trust before they can tell you what's bugging them.

Assuming that you have found a cause, you can develop strategies together with your teen for moving forward. Be warned, the best strategy for your child might not be your preferred one; you may be acutely disappointed that your lawyer-in-training wants to drop out to be a plumber (why? A plumber in the family is likely to be far more useful to you) but there is no point pushing them towards academic achievement of which they are not capable.

You may need to speak to teachers or look around at other schools or colleges for what options are out there. Perhaps they need help with studying, or maybe they have an acute 'personality clash' with their teacher. Whatever the cause, it is vital to show support for your child and respect for the way they feel. Remember that aspirations can be returned to at a later date (in our experience, returners to education are usually the most motivated and dedicated of students) – at this moment in time, your child's developing self-esteem is undoubtedly more important.

Truancy and school refusal

But what if your teen refuses to go to school at all, or, more commonly, you find out that they are skiving more often than could be reasonably excused as adolescent high jinks?

According to Government figures, truancy rose by 10% within Britain's secondary schools in 2005, so if this is worrying you, you are not likely to be alone [see report on BBC News website: http://news.bbc.co.uk/1/hi/education/4265536.stm]. As with grade-dropping, your first question should not be "How do I make my child attend school?" but "Why are they playing truant?" Possible reasons include:

- They are bored at school.

- Peer pressure – is it cool to skive?

- They are being bullied by other pupils.

- They are being picked on by a teacher.

- They are worried about not having completed homework or tests at school.

- They fail to see the value or benefit of school (e.g. have low aspirations or non-academic career goals).

- They have more attractive options that lure them from school (e.g. shopping centres, cinema, bowling, games rooms).

- They have a problem with drugs, glue-sniffing, gambling etc (see Chapter 10).

As soon as you notice a problem with regard to truancy, you

should try and find out the reasons underlying the school refusal. Let your child talk and listen to them without blaming or shouting. Encourage them to tell you why they don't want to go to school and don't fly off the handle if you don't like their explanation.

Jake's and Jennie's stories

"I lost interest in school last year. I hated one of my teachers who always picked on me. I dreaded maths tests because I always did badly. I like my mates and that was the only thing keeping me there when I went. But, to be honest, I don't see the point of school. I don't want to go to college or university – you must be joking! I want to start earning money as soon as possible and just work in a shop or something." Jake, 16

"I bunked off school a lot when I was 15. I was being picked on and bullied by some older girls and it just got easier sometimes to just slope off to the shopping centre or arcade." Jennie, 17

You should aim to develop an action plan with your truanting teen that is based on their own particular set of problems. This might involve a plan on how to tackle bullies or it might involve learning how to revise better or cope with exams (see below). It is likely to involve visiting the school or their Connexions adviser and gaining their cooperation. Sometimes half-days or some other strategy can be developed to ease your teen back into the school regime. More drastic measures may, of course, be called for and you should not dismiss the possibility of a different, more suitable school, such as a sports or technical college, or even of quitting school altogether if they are old enough.

Whatever the plan, a big part of the problem may be about you coming to terms with the fact that your child wants or needs to go in a direction that you never wanted for them. The sooner you accept this difficult fact of life, the better and the quicker you can get on with helping your child.

Helping your teen study and revise

Whilst the onus is certainly on them to buckle down to coursework and revision there is plenty that you can do to ease their way:

■ Create a suitable environment for them in which to study. They need a quiet place, a desk, clutter-free space, warmth and good lighting. This should, ideally, be the same place all the time as it allows them to feel ownership of their space but also allows a conditioning response to develop so that the mere act of sitting in their 'revision' chair triggers the cue to study.

■ Make sure that they are not disturbed by the rest of the family and limit the chores expected of them during revision times.

■ Praise them for their efforts.

■ Offer rewards for achieving work targets. Rewards could include edible treats, TV viewing, mobile top-ups, time on the computer, small gifts and evenings out with their mates.

■ Encourage your teen to draw up a revision schedule which records what they will be studying and when. Resist the temptation to do this for them – they need ownership of the plan in order to really buy into it. Make sure that they build in breaks and rewards. Ticking the session (or topic) that they have studied provides a record for them that they are building up momentum.

■ Most people have an attention span of no more than 40 minutes, so revision sessions should be divided into these manageable chunks rather than trying to sit down for a marathon three-hour slog. Your teen may prefer to intersperse the less attractive subjects with the more enjoyable ones – or just do the worst ones first and get them out of the way.

■ Make sure that your teen has time for leisure and relaxation – and especially for some form of physical exercise. Swimming, football or another sport they enjoy are vital ways for them to relieve the tension of revising. Similarly, hobbies should be kept up even within punishing revision regimes.

■ Cook them tasty and healthy meals. This will show emotional support to them – and keep them healthy.

■ Show an interest in their work. Ask them questions about what they are learning. Be impressed by their superior knowledge – this shouldn't be too difficult as they probably already knew more than you by the time they were about 10.

■ Different people have different learning styles which means that we absorb information in different ways. Encourage your child to find out what works best for them – do they learn better from auditory information (i.e. things they hear) or from visual (what they see or read)?

Perhaps they learn more by doing? You can help them adapt their revision to suit their learning style. Visual learners can read and re-read their notes, audio learners can perhaps put material onto tapes and play them (or even record them into songs – many teens have no problem learning pop song lyrics so putting the elements of the Periodic Table to a tune may make the task a doddle) whilst kinaesthetic (doing) learners might be best writing practice essays or copying out their notes.

- Don't pressure your teens to achieve. Stress that you only want them to do their best, not achieve greatness.

- Some of us are night owls, others morning larks. Let your teen decide when they work best and if this means starting after lunch and working until 2am then so be it.

Dealing with exam and school-related stress

Exams your teen is likely to face

- Year 9 (age 14): Key Stage 3: English (including reading, writing and studying a Shakespeare play), mathematics, mental arithmetic and science.

- Year 11 (age 16): GCSE exams.

- Year 12 (age 17): AS (advanced subsidiary) exams.

- Year 13 (age 18): A2 exams (the equivalent of A-levels).

It is normal for teenagers to get stressed around exam/assessment time. In fact, it's probably good practice for them because they will invariably face stress as adults and coping with life's ups and downs is a vital life skill. So, the more you can do to help them manage and cope with their stress now, the better prepared they will be for whatever life throws at them in the future.

Before you start looking at their stress, it might be a good idea to reflect for a moment about how you deal with stress. Kids learn a great deal from their home environment about coping skills and other behaviours, so if you want them to use adaptive coping skills that are good and positive, rather than maladaptive ones that are, in the long term at least, harmful, then you need to start setting a good example (see below).

Adaptive and maladaptive stress coping strategies

Adaptive or healthy ways of dealing with stress for adults might include:

- Taking exercise
- Having a relaxing bath
- Eating good food
- Writing down how you feel
- Talking to someone about your worries

Maladaptive, or unhealthy strategies include:

- Alcohol
- Smoking
- Comfort eating
- Shouting or getting aggressive

A good starting point for your teen might be to sit down with them and discuss how stress is affecting them. The following questionnaire can be used to get the discussions underway.

1 What do you understand by the term 'stress' – i.e. if somebody said that they were 'stressed' what do you think that they would be experiencing/feeling/thinking?

2 In terms of yourself, how often would you say that you generally feel stressed? (*tick one box*)

A lot of the time ☐

Quite often ☐

Just at certain times (e.g. exam times) ☐

Sometimes ☐

Hardly ever ☐

If you do ever feel stressed, what would you say are the things that make you stressed? (*tick as many as apply*).

Worrying about school ☐

Bullying ☐

Conflict with teacher ☐

Arguments with friends ☐

Pressure from your mates (e.g. to wear certain clothes, or to smoke or behave in a certain way) ☐

Exams ☐

Poor marks at school ☐

Failure to make sports teams ☐

Homework (too much/too hard) ☐

High expectation set by older brothers or sisters ☐

Parental pressure to achieve ☐

Peer teasing about glasses, dental braces,
weight etc ☐

Thinking about the future ☐

Arguments with parents/guardians ☐

Arguments with brothers/sisters ☐

Health issues ☐

Other (*please specify*)_____

If you have ticked more than one item, please put a cross against the item that gives you the most stress.

4 If you do feel stressed, what might you do about it? Try to think back to times that you have felt stressed and think about what you did to cope.

This questionnaire is a good way to start talking to your child about stress, but it is just as important for you to be on the lookout to recognise for yourself when your teen may be suffering from too much stress (remember, some stress is good for us). Watch out for the following signs:

■ Your teen might be more tearful or aggressive than usual.

■ They might be more withdrawn than usual.

■ Their eating habits might change – either eating more (comfort eating) or less.

- Your teen may be more moody than they usually are.

- Watch out for an increase in 'nervous' habits like hair-twirling, finger-tapping and nail-biting.

- Watch out too for signs of poor health that could be stress-related – increase in eczema symptoms, worsening asthma, increased susceptibility to colds, stomach upsets and so on.

Our survey said...

Only 23% of parents said that their teenagers feel no stress about exams, with 68% claiming that their children suffer a little or quite a lot of stress; 9% of teenagers are reported by their parents to feel 'very' stressed.

The teenagers in our research used a variety of good and bad coping methods to handle the school or exam stress, with the most popular response being to lose their temper. Most popular coping methods or responses to stress included:

1 Losing their temper – 61%
2 Becoming withdrawn – 42%
3 Going out (e.g. with friends) – 28%
4 Going on the internet (e.g. to distract) – 25%
5 Eating – 23%

The best way to help your child deal with stress, whether it be from coursework, exams, school or anything else, is to follow this three-part plan:

1 Help them identify their sources of stress – i.e. what

exactly is causing them to feel stressed. Use the question-naire above, and talk to them about their concerns.

2 Help them identify their maladaptive coping strategies – again using the questionnaire above.

3 Help them to swap their maladaptive strategies for health-ier ones. These could include: sports activities, talking to a friend, writing down their problems, enjoying a hot choco-late or some other treat, and even talking through their worries with you.

We now turn our attention to another aspect of school life that may be causing you concern; the next chapter deals with bul-lying – the bullied and the bullies.

Chapter 6

Bullies and the bullied

Bullying is a big issue in the playground. Last year more than 31,000 children and young people called ChildLine (see box at end of chapter) about bullying, making it the most common problem their counsellors helped young people with. According to their website, more than one in four secondary-aged pupils said they had been bullied within the last year. This chapter helps you cope when your child is being bullied, or, perhaps worse still, when they are the bully.

Sixty-nine percent of pupils who took part in a survey by Bullying Online (see box at end of chapter) said that they had been bullied in the last 12 months and 50% of those said they had been physically hurt by a bully.

Our own research for this book suggests that 48% of teenagers have been bullied.

"My daughter was bullied for a year which led to her self-harming." *Parent of 15 year old girl*

"She has suffered name calling, had stones thrown, been pushed in the corridor at school, been threatened and received abusive emails and phone calls." *Parent of 16 year old girl*

"He has been threatened with physical abuse, been tripped down the stairs, had his backpack pulled off him and suffered name-calling." *Parent of 15 year old boy*

"She has experienced name-calling, pushing and eventually leading to a physical attack in which the police became involved." *Parent of 14 year old girl*

"We had to move her to another school because the girls were so bitchy to her. There were nasty phone calls, mental bullying at school, name-calling etc. We had to get the police involved at one point." *Parent of 15 year old girl*

"Our son was bullied on and off all through school. We tried to sort it out with the parents and teachers. He hated school and couldn't wait to leave. It had a big effect on his self-esteem. Schools do not do enough about bullying." *Parent of 17 year old boy*

What do we mean by 'bullying'?

Many researchers suggest that bullying and victimisation involve actions that are repeated over a period of time – a one-off event is thus not classed as bullying. There is not really any agreed definition of what constitutes bullying behaviour but most agree that intentional harm, either mental or physical, is involved. In addition, researchers often believe that bullying involves a power imbalance with the less powerful person being repeatedly and unfairly attacked.

Types of bullying

It is easier to identify bullying by the types of behaviour involved rather than coming up with some slick definition. There are two main categories of bullying behaviour. **Direct v indirect bullying** (Olweus 1978[1]): Direct bullying consists of face-to-face confrontation and physical aggression (hitting, kicking, punching etc), whereas indirect bullying is more subtle and includes behaviours such as social exclusion (not talking to the victim), leaving children out, rumour-spreading and name-calling.

Bullies may use both direct and indirect methods but some children (and parents) can be confused as to whether the less direct approaches actually constitute bullying. If they are repeated and result in ridicule or humiliation of the child, then they probably do.

A new type of bullying has also emerged that takes advantage of new technologies: cyberbullying. This involves taunts by text or email or taking cruel or insensitive pictures on mobile phones and passing them around.

Why children bully

There are many different 'types' of bullies. Some have what is called an 'aggressive reaction pattern' which means that they have learned to react aggressively when things go wrong for them. They may have a short fuse and anger easily. It is possible that such children copy their behaviour from others (eg other siblings or parents) and do not know of an alternative way of responding. These 'aggressive' bullies are often quite popular with their peers when they are younger but this popularity often diminishes, along with academic achievement, as they get older (Olweus 1978).

Another type of bully is the more 'passive' bully. These children are less likely to initiate the attacks but actively participate once the bullying is underway. These children often do this in order to gain the approval of the more aggressive bully. It is likely that they have lower self-esteem and thus seek to win the friendship of the more confident aggressive bully by joining in.

Parental upbringing can have an impact on whether children become bullies, but it is important to note that this only accounts for some of the bullies. Parents cannot and should not be automatically blamed if their child bullies. However, Olweus (1980[2]) has identified some parental factors that can have an influence:

- Parents who are less emotionally warm and involved with their children can increase the aggressiveness and hostility that their child later displays.

- Parents who are more tolerant of aggressive behaviour at home (e.g. with siblings) can lead to children having less clear boundaries about the acceptability of aggressive acts.

- Parents who use more physical punishments and violent outbursts as a way of controlling their child at home can teach their child that this is the correct way to respond when things don't go their way.

Who is bullied?

Olweus (1991[3]) suggested that there are two main types of victim: passive or provocative. Passive victims are far more common and these children are probably a little more anxious and insecure than other children (factors that are noticed by the bully). They are often quite cautious and may have lower self-esteem (Neary and Joseph 1994[4]) and again, it is these facets that are noted by the bully. Passive victims may have fewer friends for one reason or another (which adds to their lowered self-esteem), perhaps they are new at school or they may lack confidence in social interactions.

Provocative victims are less common but these children are both anxious and aggressive. They behave in ways that create tension and irritation in their peers. They may have unusual behaviour patterns that provoke amusement in their peers and are more likely to react emotionally to minor problems and upsets.

Gender differences in bullying behaviours

According to researchers (e.g. Bjorkqvist, Lagerspetz and Kaukainen, 1992[5]) boys are generally more likely to use direct, physical forms of bullying while girls tend to bully in groups and use more indirect forms, which is harder to detect and prove. It is thought that the reason for this is that for boys, physical dominance and hierarchy is important among their peers, but girls are more concerned with relationships and friendship issues. Boys may also bully in order to obtain power and to prove their superiority whereas girls may bully in order to affirm that they are part of the 'in crowd' – by excluding others they affirm their status with their friends.

It is thought that there is more bullying among boys than girls but this may be due to the fact that girls' bullying behaviour is less likely to be classed as such. Direct bullying is easier to observe so it is possible that girls' bullying is underestimated and under-reported. Girls are likely to be bullied by either gender but boys tend to be bullied by other boys (Drake et al 2003[6]).

When is bullying most likely to occur?

The transition period from primary to secondary school is the most significant time in terms of childhood bullying. At this time, children start going through puberty at different rates, leading to differences in size, strength and physical development. This leads to some children becoming more vulnerable due to advanced or delayed changes, as well as giving others advantages in terms of strength, size and so on. At the same time, the nature of conflict resolution is changing as children enter adolescence; social awareness, concerns about social status, peer influence – all these factors start playing important roles in relationships at school. A study of phone calls made to ChildLine (which offers children advice on any problems) showed that the peak ages for callers ringing about bullying problems was around 11-14 years (Macleod and Morris 1996[7]).

In addition, at this time, children start new schools and have to form new friendships and social groups. This can leave many feeling insecure or threatened as they struggle to establish their role in the new hierarchies that develop.

The good news is that bullying does tend to decrease throughout the adolescent years (Smith et al 2004[8]). This may be due to the fact that older kids tend to pick on the newer children or that as children get older, they become more resistant to being bullied, settle into new schools and develop new circles of friends. The bad news, however, is that bullying within older adolescence tends to be more severe (Sullivan, Cleary and Sullivan 2004[9]).

What does bullying do to a child?

According to Coastkid [Brighton and Hove's anti-bullying web-site **www.coastkid.org**] children who are bullied:

- Can be so depressed or stressed they actually become ill
- Can have really low self-esteem
- Can become shy and withdrawn
- Can develop physical complaints, like constant stomach aches and headaches, which are brought on by stress

Is your teen being bullied?

Few teens will come right out and claim they are being bullied. Many don't realise that this is what is happening, especially with indirect bullying, and others are embarrassed or afraid to admit it. Signs then to watch out for include:

- Reluctance to go to school
- Reluctance to catch usual school bus or take usual route
- Playing truant

- Grade slipping

- Hostility or moodiness at home

- Complaining of illness with no obvious symptoms

- 'Losing' possessions

- Not eating school lunches (either to avoid bullies or because their money is being stolen)

- Lacking confidence and being withdrawn

- Becoming aggressive with siblings

- Coming home with cuts or bruises

What to do if your child is being bullied

If you think your child might be being bullied at school (or on the way to school) here are some of the steps that you can consider:

- Talk to your teen about their worries if you suspect all is not well. Stay calm and encourage them to share their problems.

- Keep a record of any incidents that occur, however minor they may seem.

- Identify the likely triggers and sites of the abuse. For example, does the bullying occur on the school bus, in the changing rooms, at lunchtime?

- Look at ways that your child can avoid the trigger situations if possible. For example, can they request to move seats in the classroom? Take a different route home?

These are avoidance strategies and don't attack the problem head-on, but may reassure your child if they are nervous about anything more confrontational.

■ Teach your teen to be assertive and 'stand up' to the bullies. Bullies love to cause fear and get a reaction; if your child can stop this reaction, the bully will lose interest. Ways in which they can do this include:

Looking the bully in the eye and saying No very firmly and possibly following this with an alternative suggestion such as "Shall we go and play football together now?" or just walking away.

Using the 'broken record' technique, saying the same sentence over and over again, particularly useful when someone isn't listening to you.

Saying nothing, possibly smiling and just walking away.

If there is a group of bullies, encourage your teen to speak to one or two of the less active members on their own and ask them why they are acting like this. Without the support of their mates, bullies may well feel ashamed if they see the effect their behaviour is having.

■ Many children will be reluctant for you to speak to the school for fear of reprisals. But you can ask them about their anti-bullying policy – every school should have one.

■ Avoid shouting or accusing a young bully. This may well make the bully defensive and take it out on your child.

■ Try and instil confidence in your teen by praising them and encouraging them in activities they are good at.

- Encourage them to attend activities, classes or to pursue hobbies. This will enhance their self-esteem and give them access to potential friends away from the bullies.

- Ask them to write a list of their positive traits – what they are good at, what nice qualities they have – all positive, self-affirming stuff.

- Spend more time with them. They are feeling vulnerable so they need you to be around. Sometimes they will want to talk at odd moments, such as when you're in the car or washing up (see Chapter 3), not necessarily just when you schedule time for them to talk to you.

- With incidents of cyberbullying, keep nasty texts or emails for evidence, however tempting it is to destroy them.

- Plan treats and fun for your teen. Let them see that life ain't all bad!

In more severe cases, the school will have to be involved, but what should your school be doing? Good anti-bullying policies should include anonymous reporting of problems, mentor schemes and specially trained adults that kids can turn to for help.

Racist bullying

If your child is being picked on, bullied or discriminated against because of their race, colour, religion or culture, then this can introduce different elements into the equation. They might be taunted because of their clothes, because they need time off school for religious festivals, or peers may make racist or derogatory gestures (such as a Nazi salute), bring in racist materials (such as magazines and articles) or make racist 'jokes'. Bullying Online has some excellent advice (see box at end of chapter) including contacting the Commission for Racial Equality and the police.

Homophobic bullying

One of the most prevalent forms of bullying occurs because of sexuality, or perceived sexuality. DfES research showed that most teachers were aware of the issue with 82% saying they were aware of verbal incidents and 26% of physical incidents. If a school does not have a holistic approach to dealing with homophobia, then such incidents will occur more often and pupils will not recognise it is unacceptable.

Whether or not your child is gay or lesbian, they may be a victim of homophobic bullying and be at the receiving end of insults or physical abuse. You should expect your school to work with parents and carers as well as the wider community to ensure they have effective policies and procedures in place. You can get more information in the DfES publication, *Stand up for us: Challenging homophobia in schools*, downloadable at **www.wiredforhealth.gov.uk/PDF/stand_up_for_us_04.pdf**

What if it is your child who is the bully?

Teenagers who bully often do so because they feel insecure, threatened or jealous in some way. Perhaps they have been bullied in the past and think that they are best doing the bullying before they get picked on again. The best approach is a 'no-blame' one – try not to yell or shout at them, or punish them with sanctions (such as grounding them); this does not really tackle the reason for their behaviour, which may well become even worse.

Instead, you need to challenge their behaviour in a supportive way. Ask them questions about why they are bullying. Is it to get attention? To make themselves feel better? Do they like the power? Do they like hurting people? Are they worried or upset about anything? Is anyone else picking on them? Are they frightened? Are they trying to keep 'in' with their pals?

Help them to see the world from the perspective of their victim. Ask them how they imagine their victim is feeling. Perhaps even ask the victim to come round after school and explain the effect your child's behaviour has on them.

Extra help

For help, advice or information on anything in this chapter, contact Kidscape, a national charity aimed at preventing and dealing with bullying. They have a helpline, 08451 205 204 Monday-Friday from 10am-4pm. Also, check out their website which includes plenty of downloadable guides and advice at **www.kidscape.org.uk**

Another excellent port of call is ChildLine. Children and young people can call them on 0800 1111 about problems they are experiencing with bullying. They too have excellent resources on their website: **www.childline.org.uk**

Bullying Online is a charity founded in 1999 and has excellent resources. Check them out at **www.bullying.co.uk**

Thanks to Aimee Peacock for contributing to parts of this chapter.

Chapter 7

Sex, lies and puberty

"During the hormonal and bodily turmoil the most important question most teenagers ask is 'Am I normal?' but they frequently don't believe you when you try to reassure them that they are. Unfortunately, the biological development does not always go hand in hand with the emotional maturity. The gap in modern society between the arrival of the sexual urges and social adulthood can create major problems." *Parent of two teenagers*

There is no doubting that the issue most parents are either uncomfortable or embarrassed about discussing with their children is sex (actually, our research suggests that masturbation specifically is the most cringe-inducing – see page 105). Invariably parents report children knowing more about sex than they do or they have an expectation that schools will deal with education on the issue. But parents can have a vital role in dealing with issues on a one-to-one basis, away from peer pressure and from the values of unknown others. In other words, this is your job – don't let embarrassment stop you.

This chapter will look at the practicalities of doing this and the knowledge you may need. It will help you play a positive role in influencing your child and not fall into the many traps that are easily encountered. We will look at the trials of puberty; the worries about appearance and behaviour and the anguish and joy of romantic, intimate and, yes, even sexual relationships.

Most importantly, we will stress the need to treat all these changes as opportunities to engage positively with your child and to confidently develop your relationship with them.

Our survey said...

We asked parents how they deal with sex education with their teenagers. The most common response (69%) is to engage in "frank and ongoing discussion". Around 14% give their children reading material while 6% chicken out and leave the matter entirely to the school.

The sexual issue that parents feel most comfortable talking to their teenagers about is contraception (56%). There is a big gender difference, with 70% of parents feeling comfortable discussing this with girls compared with 44% feeling comfortable with boys *.

The next most 'comfortable' issue is menstruation, with just over half parents saying they feel very comfortable talking about this. Not surprisingly, perhaps, there was a big gender difference, with 77% of parents feeling comfortable talking about this to girls compared with just 31% to boys.

Discussing sex is comfortable for 36% of parents (again, they felt more comfortable with girls than with boys) but the most uncomfortable topic is masturbation, with only 16% of parents feeling comfortable discussing this with their teenagers.

* **These gender differences may reflect the likelihood that more mothers than fathers completed the surveys.**

Physical development – helping your child through the changes

Before being able to support your teenager through their transition from child to adult, it is important to know what changes they will be going through. You will, of course, be pretty much aware of half the changes, since you will have gone through them yourself.

The physical changes can usually start anywhere between the ages of about eight to 13 for a girl and nine to 14 for a boy. However, there are even variations beyond this and neither you, nor your child, should be concerned if they start puberty early or late. As a guide, puberty will often occur at around the same time it did for the parent of the same sex, but this should not be an expectation.

Boys – the main physical changes boys will notice are:

- Hair growth around penis, testes, underarms, chest, legs and face. This will normally be quite fine at first. Often the first appearance is on the top lip and, at some point, boys will want to shave their face. You can offer to buy them their first shaver. They will usually prefer an electric shaver as there is less chance of getting cut. You can also reassure them about the normality of their hair growth, particularly if they are an early or late developer.

- Lowering of the voice pitch, known as the voice breaking. Unless they are a singer, this should not be of too much concern, although it can be embarrassing at times. They may find their voice difficult to control for a few weeks but you can reassure them that it will pass.

■ Growth in size of testes and penis. Do be aware that one testicle being larger than the other is perfectly normal and this is easy to reassure your child about.

■ Acne, particularly around the face, neck and shoulders, due to the skin becoming oilier. You may discuss washing more frequently (although not obsessively). Hair may also become greasier and need washing more frequently.

■ Body odour as a result of the sweat glands becoming more active. You may want to give them a gift of some anti-per-spirant but a discussion with them before offering the solution may prove more fruitful.

■ Shoulders get wider.

■ Muscles get bigger and stronger as your son grows taller.

■ Wet dreams may occur. This is secretion of semen, not urine, and is perfectly normal. You may just need to wash their sheets slightly more often.

■ Involuntary erections may occur due to excitement, nervousness or for no reason at all. This lack of control can be unnerving for a boy and giving them prior knowledge can certainly help maintain their self-esteem.

Girls – the main physical changes girls will notice are:

■ Growth in size of breasts, vagina and labia. Usually the first sign of puberty will be a girl noticing her breasts 'budding'.

Breasts can grow at different rates and so be different sizes. This is perfectly normal. If it is causing concern, your child should see a doctor or other health professional.

■ Hair growth around pubic area and underarms. Hair on arms and legs darkens. Possibility of hair on upper lip darkening. Girls may want to shave or depilate their legs. You can offer to buy them a shaver or depilatories. The latter may be preferable as there is less chance of getting cut. They may also want to depilate or lighten facial hair and you could discuss the options with them. You can also reassure them as to the normality of their hair growth, particularly if they are an early or late developer.

■ A whitish or clear vaginal discharge is normal for many girls.

■ Menstruation, commonly called periods, begins. These will probably be light at first and will become heavier over the first year. They may also be irregular for the first few months. There may be some cramping prior to the period, which may be eased through gentle exercise.

"It is often useful to share your own period problems to show daughters that you are both women and you do understand. As family menstrual cycles tend to coincide a certain amount of sympathy for each other's moods, pains, tiredness etc is also a way of forming a close relationship." *Mother of teenage girl*

■ Acne, particularly around the face, neck and shoulders, due to the skin becoming oilier. You may discuss washing more frequently (although not obsessively). Hair may also become greasier and need washing more frequently.

■ Body odour as a result of the sweat glands becoming more active. You may want to give them a gift of some anti-perspirant but a discussion with them before offering the solution may prove more fruitful.

■ Hips get wider and weight is gained here.

■ Leg muscles get bigger and stronger as your daughter grows taller.

Talking about puberty

As with all communication, you should plan some time away from distractions to discuss these issues. However, it may be that an issue suddenly arises and you need to deal with it immediately. In this scenario, it is even more important to keep calm and be prepared to listen and ask questions rather than state your opinion.

You should be prepared to use your personal recollections, especially if you are the same gender, and share the fact that your child's development is likely to follow the same course as yours. You should, however, ensure you get more knowledge by reading around the subject. The more knowledge you have, the more you can share it with them and give them more confidence as you will be more confident.

The overview of the changes above will give you some basic knowledge but it is worth visiting websites such as **www.puberty101.com** to ensure that you have as much knowledge as possible so that you can exude as much confidence as possible.

In an encounter with your child, your role should be to enable them to find answers for themselves. Do not feel as if you have to tell them what to do (such as what type of sanitary protection to use). You will get far more positive results from comments such as, "If that's what you feel you need to do, I'll help you," than "I don't think you're ready for that yet."

Image – dealing with worries over personal appearance, hygiene and other self-esteem problems

"The awakening awareness of the opposite sex leads to a disturbing preoccupation with appearance, weight, height, size of sexual organs and so on. Body odour changes from the nasty sweaty stage to the over-use of body sprays which I have choked on frequently." *Parent of two teenagers*

It is almost inevitable that your child will become concerned about their appearance as they develop through adolescence. Indeed, 38% of parents in our survey cited this as one of the main issues that they thought their teenagers were worried about. The physical reasons for this are because of the changes taking place in their bodies. But alongside this will be the uncertainty brought on by the hormonal changes that are happening and the lack of control they feel over their body's development.

There is also clear evidence that the way the media, particularly television, portrays body image leads to body dissatisfaction in both genders.[10] In recent years this has clearly had an increasing influence on young men as incidence of eating disorders among males has grown. Nevertheless, the rate of eating disorders among females is still much higher (see next chapter).

"Her self-confidence about her looks is below zero and preventing her living life to the full. It breaks my heart as she is very beautiful but can't see it herself." *Parent of 17 year old girl.*

Clearly, as a parent, you would not want your child to suffer from an eating disorder. So avoiding comments about their weight, either in terms of criticising being overweight but also overly complimenting slimness, is important. However, positive comments about other elements of your teenager's being, as long as they sound genuine, will help enhance their self-esteem.

It is absolutely imperative that you avoid making negative comments about your teenager's personal appearance. This could be the most difficult biting of your tongue you ever do as, for example, your daughter decides to wear a very revealing outfit or your son starts to grow his hair over his eyes. So, if you shouldn't make negative comments, how can you help your child make positive decisions about their image?

The answer lies in framing your suggestions in questions, particularly open ones, and getting your teenager to answer these questions for themselves. Open questions are those that cannot be answered Yes or No and begin with one of the following six words: Who, Why, What, When, Where and How.

Here are a couple of examples:
You want to say: "You look awful with that baseball cap."
You actually say: "What look are you trying to get across?"

The tone in which you speak is just as important and you need to keep it neutral, so it is not perceived as criticism. In this example, you may just get grunts or something along the lines of "It's a cool look." A response that supports their judgment: "If you feel cool like that then that's fine by me," may not produce immediate change but will make them feel supported and open them up to a further discussion around fashion sense and, possibly, independence from the 'expected' image.

You want to say: "Sanitary towels will be more comfortable because I found it really difficult using tampons."

You actually say: "How comfortable do you find tampons as opposed to towels?"

With the right tone, this could be the start of a positive conversation about sanitary protection. Again, even a short answer will give you the opportunity to support them: "If you feel more comfortable with tampons then I'll buy those for you." This may lead to a further discussion or not but it does provide the opportunity for your daughter to be supported.

With this approach you need to be prepared for your child to disagree and you must decide where your boundaries lie. For example, if you do object to piercing, you need to make this clear to your teenager but ensure they still have the opportunity to give their opinion and be listened to. If they get angry, you need to remain calm and stress that, while you understand their wants, you are their parent and this is an issue where you have a clear limit.

Hygiene

Our survey said...

Personal hygiene, such as not showering enough, is cited as a source of conflict between parents and teenagers by 9% of our survey sample.

One of the consequences of puberty, described above, is that hygiene becomes an issue. Your child may or may not be aware of this and so it is important to ensure they understand the importance of keeping clean, in terms of physical appearance and odour – spots and smells. For girls, this extends to cleanliness associated with menstruation.

Ensuring your child has the facts about puberty will make their decisions about hygiene easier. You can offer to buy whichever anti-perspirant, soap or sanitary protection they ask for, giving them some level of control while still being part of the process. They may ask for the money instead and you will need to decide if you are willing to give them this level of control as it removes an opportunity to engage with them – but allows them to make their own choices.

If they begin to get lax about hygiene, finding a planned space to discuss their issues is the best way to get them back on track. You should clearly avoid passing comments or curt remarks.

You need to be clear that you will change their sheets more often. Also that, if they need you to change them for whatever reason, e.g. sperm or menstrual fluid (and they probably won't want to tell you what the reason is – see the parent's comment below), you are happy to do so when they request it. If you do their washing, this is easy to put into practice. If they are expected to do their own, you will need to have a discussion with them as to how they will implement this and make a clear agreement.

Behaviour

"The chances of a boy telling you his sheets need changing due to seminal fluid are less than zero. I just went in his room when he was at school and stripped the bed when necessary without any comment." *Parent of teenage boy*

Physiological changes also affect behaviour. Hormones can influence sexual motivations but just as important is pubertal development. There is no doubt that these lead to masturbation but not necessarily to sexual activity. The latter is related to many other factors young people face socially.[11] It is unclear whether the belief that depression or mood swings increase during puberty is true. This clearly varies substantially among adolescents and your concern will be with your child.[12]

You should remember that the way your teenager behaves is a result of a whole combination of factors, both physical and mental, and, therefore, be careful not to just focus on the behaviour they are presenting. Since the cumulative, simultaneous life events of puberty, school, peer and family changes are argued to have an effect on social competence,[13] your ability to take all this into account can reap rewards in building your relationship with your teenager.

Some researchers believe that adolescents are able to cope with the potentially stressful change with relative stability by dealing with one issue at a time.[14] Those who must deal with more than one problem at a time are those in whom problems are most likely to occur. So don't put too much on your child. Deal with issues one at a time. Keep focused. This may mean putting other issues aside to be dealt with another time, but solving one problem is usually a big enough achievement in one conversation. In order to recall all the issues that arise, you may even want to make a note of them, and possibly share that with your teenager when the time is right.

Always try and respond to your child sensitively and show them through your words and body language that you empathise with them. That this requires a great deal of patience and self-control is undoubtedly true, but the consequences of being confrontational could be far worse. The worst that could happen by not confronting them is that they say you are soft. However, if you link your sensitive approach with clear rules that you have set early on in the teenage years, you should be able to get the balance of control and empowerment right.

Delayed development

For teenagers, the issue of Delayed Puberty can be distressing. Puberty is considered to be delayed if it has not occurred by the age of 13 in girls and 14 in boys. If your teenager does have Delayed Puberty, they should have a full evaluation by a paediatrician.

If the whole process of puberty has not been completed in four to five years, or if menstruation has not started for a girl by the age of 16, this may also be considered Delayed Puberty.

Most children with Delayed Puberty are perfectly healthy and just have a delay in their growth and development. Since genetics influences the timing of puberty, if other family members were also delayed, this can explain their delay and you can reassure them. Some may, however, have issues with sex hormones (oestrogen or testosterone) not being secreted properly. If this is the case, your paediatrician should be able to prescribe appropriate treatment.

Since any delay in puberty is observable, you will have every opportunity to mitigate the psychological effects it can have. You should be aware that, however positive you may be towards your child, they may still be frustrated and embarrassed by the perception that they are less mature than their peers. You can look to mitigate this by giving them other opportunities to emphasis their maturity, such as allowing them to buy their own clothes or make decisions about the décor of their room.

Girls whose development is delayed may wish to buy padded bras and even buy sanitary protection. Using the technique of asking questions, you can help your daughter make positive decisions on such issues. Within this, you may want to ask questions about honesty, so that this is considered properly.

Sex

It is always worth remembering that the reason for puberty is to prepare us for being sexually active and, for most, procreation. The hormonal changes that occur lead to adolescent males and females developing a sex drive that they have not had previously. This can have a number of consequences for your teenager:

- They can be disconcerted by the urges they feel, which can lead to them becoming withdrawn or displaying irrational behaviour. Initially, you need to ensure they understand why these changes are occurring, giving them a better chance to deal with them. As time goes on, you may need to be very understanding of their behaviour and then reinforce their understanding of why they feel as they do.

- Embarrassment may be felt because of sexual arousal occurring at inopportune moments. This is particularly true for young males because they may not be able to control their erections. While this may make for an amusing sketch in a sit-com, the reality is not so funny. Obviously, if they are aware of why this is happening, they are less likely to be embarrassed, so giving them this information should be seen as part of your parental responsibility.

- Your teenager may develop a crush on an older individual (and not always of the opposite sex), such as a teacher or youth worker, possibly because they are seen as caring, as mature or unobtainable. This can lead to embarrassment or, sometimes, to inappropriate, promiscuous behaviour. While you may hope that those in positions of authority would always deal with such situations promptly and sensitively, this will not necessarily be the case. As always, discussing such issues with your teenager before they occur is the best way to manage them. You can look out for abruptness when talking about school or youth groups, but be aware that such abruptness may be for other reasons. Obviously, you are able to talk to teachers, youth workers and other professionals in confidence, so don't be afraid to ask them how things are going and raise any concerns.

■ Frustration can be particularly difficult for the teenager who cannot fulfil their sexual urges. The usual way they would deal with this is through masturbation, and the majority of both sexes do relieve themselves in this way. Again, forewarned is forearmed so you need to be ready to have a discussion with them about this early on in their adolescence.

You will not be alone if you disapprove of your 16 year old engaging in sex, along with smoking and drug-taking, on the grounds of morals and health implications.[15] Where young people do conform to your views or rules, this will usually be achieved through reward rather than sanction. Where they encounter moral proscription, youngsters deciding to act counter to this will frequently resort to secrecy.

You may also be faced with the situation where your child is engaging in sex before 16. While sex before 16 is illegal in the UK (before 17 in Northern Ireland), the reality does not reflect this. Research suggests that between one in five and one in three young people under 16 years old are sexually active.[16]

As a parent you need to brace yourself for the real possibility that your child may be having sex much earlier than you may like. However, you should also realise that you, along with three-quarters of parents,[17] may not be aware if your child is having sex. What you need to avoid is being one of the 80% of parents wanting teachers to deal with these issues[18] rather than doing so yourself.

It is also likely that your child will find out a lot about sex from many sources other than yourself. While you would hope that school would be the main source, your teenager's knowledge may, to a greater or lesser extent, come from their peers, siblings, magazines, television and, more frequently nowadays, the internet. Some of this learning will be factual and some very misinformed.

Several of these sources will include pornography and there is certainly increasing ease of access to pornography for children with the growth of internet use. Since much pornography also paints a very unrealistic picture of sex, this can lead to more confusion on the part of your child.

Based on this, you need to make sure that your knowledge is up-to-date and accurate, and not based on some of the fallacies you may have been presented with in your life. The resources at the end of this chapter may be some help.

What to say and how to say it

"I have tried discussing sexual issues with him but I think he was more embarrassed than me." *Mother of 14 year old boy*

"I was aware that my teenagers were often more clued up on sex than they thought I was, so it was important not to patronise them. I broached the subject by saying I was not going to give them a speech but that I hoped they had respect for themselves and they never felt used or dirty after encounters with the opposite sex. It was amazing what came out when they acknowledged that I was trusting them to make their own decisions." *Parent of two teenagers*

Dealing with the development of sexual awareness may seem daunting but you are very capable of doing so. The first thing to remember is that you have been through it yourself. While it may be uncomfortable, it is very worthwhile thinking back to your first sexual experiences before discussing the issue with your teenager. The more at ease you feel about the subject, the more at ease you will seem to your child.

The more you can get your child to talk in a conversation about sex, the better. Don't be afraid to ask the sensitive questions: "Have you had sex?" and "Are you using contraception?" but make sure you that your tone is level, not accusing, and your body language is open (no arm-crossing!). If you are asking open questions, you are in control of the conversation and able to help your child open up. You will need to use everything you have learned about positive body language – nodding as they talk, smiling with them and so on – to get them to feel comfortable but you will get your reward when they allow you into their thoughts.

Of course, whatever you say and however you say it, your teenager may still not want to open up or still tell you that you don't understand what they are going through. The reality is that parents and their adolescents often hold similar values but adolescents perceive that their parents' views are more different from their own than they actually are.[19] Your only recourse in breaking through these barriers is patience. There is no point entering into an argument or resorting to punishments. You need to carry on using your complete set of communication tools and believe that your child will, eventually, respond.

As sexual awareness increases, so does the range of issues that you will be faced with. Dealing with catching your child masturbating (an unsurprisingly frequent occurrence when you consider it is an activity undertaken by the majority of the population and quite frequently by many teenagers) will seem easy once you get to dealing with the more emotional highs and lows of relationships.

Where patience is needed in talking about sex, this is even truer when taking on issues that require emotional awareness. It is much easier, although possibly embarrassing, to deal with physical issues that your teenager can at least understand, than the feelings that come with their emotional attachment to another person. As always, sharing your experiences may be useful but your listening skills, allowing your teenager space to talk without any criticism, will be more valuable. You should also be prepared to give unconditional support to your child, regardless of whether you feel they may be at fault. If they are prepared to open up on such an issue to you, it is imperative that you do not push them away with criticism.

Sexual orientation

So far, we have made no assumptions about whether your teenager will be straight, gay or bisexual. This is important because we are not going to, and neither should you.

Whatever your attitudes towards homosexuality or heterosexuality, it is important not to make assumptions about this in relation to your child. This is because, if you do have a negative attitude towards homosexuality, and your child is gay, this will serve as a barrier to you successfully communicating with them and, potentially, alienate them. The reality you must deal with is that, whatever you do, you are not going to change the sexuality of your child. So why try?

"He's still our son and we would accept it [if he told us he was gay]. As long as he's happy, that's all that matters." *Parent of 16 year old boy*

"To be honest, I'd be very upset but I would have to accept it." *Parent of 18 year old boy*

"I'd be worried because it's a difficult path because so many people are still anti-gay." *Parent of 15 year old girl*

"I wouldn't be bothered at all and often discuss this with my daughter." *Parent of 15 year old girl.*

"I'd be sad for the loss of the life I had envisioned for her. It would take a considerable amount of time to grieve for the future she now wouldn't have –grandchildren, wedding and so on." *Mother of 15 year old girl*

"She's my daughter and I love her unconditionally so it wouldn't bother me." *Parent of teenager*

"I would be disappointed. I would feel happier if she was in a normal man/woman relationship." *Parent of 16 year old girl*

"We think he is gay but he won't admit it. We've said we are fine about it." *Parent of 18 year old boy*

"It would be another nail in the coffin if she was gay." *Parent of 16 year old girl*

What is important to be clear about is the discrimination that a young gay man, lesbian or bisexual will face in society. If

your child does come out to you as not being straight, this is
something you should be able to talk to them about, showing
them that you care about their well-being, whatever you think
of their sexuality.

More difficult are issues such as cross-dressing or transgen-
derism. While you may have difficulty dealing with such
issues, this will be minor compared to what a teenager who is
confused by such feelings will be going through. Again,
whether or not you are open-minded is not the issue. You just
need to give your child space to talk to you and be as accept-
ing as possible, while showing appropriate parental concern.

What you may also need in circumstances like these, where
you have difficulty dealing with the issues, is support from
others in the same situation. Families and Friends of Lesbians
and Gays [**www.fflag.org.uk**] is set up to do just that with
telephone helplines and meetings to help you support your
children, with love and pride.

Risky behaviour

It is highly likely that your teenager will engage in behaviour
to a greater or lesser extent that puts them at risk. While the
causal effect is not proved, young people engaging in one set of
risky behaviours – such as abusing alcohol or drugs – may do
so in others.

Young people are aware of the need to manage the risks associated with their behaviour but do not always seek the right
advice that is being provided by official agencies such as
school.[20] As a parent, you need to help your child to manage
their risks by being up front with factual information that you

are able to present to them without prejudice. Discussing risks of their behaviour can be a positive way to approach issues your child is dealing with.

Both genders find risks enjoyable but young men report being far less afraid of risks than young women.[21] You need to keep this in mind when talking with your teenager.

You should also ensure that your child knows about sexually transmitted diseases so they can manage their risk behaviour. Your providing this information also opens up communication channels and, providing you can talk about it without embarrassment, should lead to increased mutual respect. But, providing people with Aids information, for example, does not by itself influence behaviour.[22] You need to be prepared to discuss sex honestly with your children in order to properly smooth their transition to adulthood.

The reality is that less than 20% of adolescents' sex education comes from mothers and only around 2% from fathers.[23] In those families where children can talk freely and openly with parents about sex, the children are less likely to be sexually active.[24] By opening up the communication channels and being prepared to discuss issues about sex *with* your teenager, rather than telling them what they should be doing, you will be far more likely to help them engage in sex responsibly.

You need to be aware of where your teenager is getting their knowledge from. According to one source, school-based health classes, including teaching aids such as pamphlets and videos, consistently rank as the primary source of contraceptive, birth control and pregnancy prevention information among adolescents.[25] This being the case, you need to fully engage with your child's school and, at the very least, make sure that you have as much information as they do. Guidance given to schools tells them that they should work in partnership with parents when planning and delivering sex and relationship education.[26] So make sure that they discuss with you what they are delivering and that you are happy with it. You can then plan how you will complement this (or how this will complement what you are doing) at home.

You should also recognise that 'teaching' sexual health will rarely put the issues in an emotional or relationship context. As the parent, you have the opportunity to do this, not by being overly moody about the issue but by balancing the facts with the feelings that will occur when two people look to engage in sex. If you are able to be open with your teenager, and share your feelings about sex, they should be more comfortable opening up to you.

One of the key issues you will need to discuss with your teenager is condom use. In an environment where STDs are prevalent, condoms are the best way, after abstinence, of protection from catching a disease. Add to that the fact that they protect against pregnancy, and you can make a good sales pitch for their use. For lesbians, the issue still exists and femidoms, however fiddly, should still be recognised as an effective barrier against STDs.

How important is it for you to have this discussion? You need to remember that most young people do not use condoms routinely. Hatherall et al (2005) found that two-thirds of those aged 16-21 reported using condoms inconsistently for vaginal sex. Consistent use of barrier forms of contraception for oral and anal sex was also worryingly low.[27] Such facts should focus you on protecting your child and ensuring that their behaviour does not risk their health.

Extra help

While you may feel that the world has changed and teenagers know far more about sex than they did when you were one, the reality is that there are also many more resources for you to use. Don't be afraid to get hold of books and leaflets to facilitate your discussions with your teenager.

Some useful resources are:

The Sex Files, Jasminka Petrovic, Book House, Brighton, 2000. A very accessible book, amusingly illustrated, covering all areas of growing up, sex and relationships.

Two's Company? The Reverend Jane Fraser, Brook Publications, Oxford, 1997. Useful pack looking at relationships that you can adapt to use with your child.

Strides: A practical guide to sex and relationships education with young men, Simon Blake and Joanna Laxton, Family Planning Association, London, 1998. Good information that you can adapt to use with your son.

Sense: Sex and Relationships, Simon Blake and Louise Orpin, Sense Interactive CDs/National Children's Bureau, London, 2003. Interactive CD-ROM with a parents/carers booklet pack. Clear information and practical advice on all aspects of sex and relationships.

4You, 4Girls, 4Boys, Family Planning Association, London, 2001. Accessible comic-style information leaflets.

www.puberty101.com – website operated by teenagers for teenagers but with questions answered by professionals.

www.ruthinking.co.uk – advice on sex, relationships and contraception linked to Sexwise confidential phone advice service on 0800 28 29 30.

www.thesite.org – clear information and guidance for teenagers on sex and relationships, run by YouthNet UK.

Chapter 8

Family relationships

*T*heir social life is central to teenagers – as are their blossoming romantic liaisons. But their relationship with family members – parents, grandparents and siblings – is the backbone that keeps it all together. This chapter focuses on several aspects of family life that may be cause for concern.

Healthy family relationships

A healthy family relationship at home can have enormous benefits for the mental health of your developing adolescent. But what exactly does that mean? Does this mean that you can't get angry? That siblings shouldn't fight? That 'broken' families are a big no-no?

A healthy set of family relationships may include the following features;

- Parents do get angry with their teens, but are usually able to deal with things in a calm and appropriate way (most of the time!)

- Parents are not abusive to their children (for example, by belittling them, hurting them mentally or physically).

- Siblings do fight and argue but will protect each other to people outside the family (such as sticking up for each other in the playground).

- The family unit may be 'fractured' but the children are being put first in any difficulties that are experienced.

- Children feel able to talk to a family member about their problems.

- Families eat together at the table several times a week.

- Children receive frequent praise from their parents.

- Parents, whether they live together or not, show an interest in their child's school and social life.

The influence of an absent father/parent

According to the National Father Initiative [**www.stolen children.net**] in America, having an absent father is grim news for children:

- Fatherless children are more likely to drop out of school.

- Fatherless daughters are more likely to become pregnant as teenagers.

- Children whose father doesn't live with them are more likely to score lower on tests of achievement.

- The absence of a father contributes to juvenile delinquency.

But is it really all such bad news? Are all teenagers doomed to a life of underachievement when dad leaves home? The answer, as many single parents will no doubt testify, is surely no. The way that the absence is dealt with, the involvement of the absent parent, the attitude of both parents … all these can be significant factors in the effects on your child.

Fathers (or, less commonly, mothers) can be 'absent' for a number of reasons including divorce, death or imprisonment. And, for divorce, there are degrees of 'absence' ranging from the absent parent having no contact whatsoever with the child, to hosting frequent visits and sleepovers. The parent may have been absent for many years or the situation may be a new one for your teenager to cope with.

Because the situations can vary so much, it is difficult to produce a blanket plan of action for coping with an absent parent. Instead, we will focus on two of the more common scenarios: that of a totally absent divorced father and that of the involved father (or mother) who no longer lives in the family home.

1 Totally/almost absent parent

In this situation, the parent has all but disappeared from their child's life; contact may be sporadic, or occasional, but the absent parent plays little or no role in the day-to-day lives of their teens. The absent parent might live some distance away (even another country), may have another family or may even be in prison. Each situation brings its own difficulties for the developing adolescent (who, we must remember, is struggling to achieve their own sense of self and worth against this backdrop), which may include the following:

A feeling of being let down by the absent parent. For a parent, watching your child face disappointment after disappointment as their father (or mother) fails to meet scheduled arrangements, forgets birthdays or repeatedly cancels visits at the last minute is hugely tough. For the teen going through this, it can be soul-destroying. Their fragile sense of worth is intimately tied up in how significant others view them and how they are treated is, they believe, an accurate reflection of their worth. It is hard for teenagers not to feel rejected by such a parent and such feelings can either be externalised (this isn't about me – it's my dad who is the idiot) or internalised (my dad treats me like this because I am boring/unworthy/horrible).

"My daughter is frequently let down by her dad. He makes promises he doesn't keep and arrangements he doesn't stick to. I feel that my daughter thinks it is her fault – that if she were funnier or prettier he would be more interested. She tries so hard to win his approval so as to maintain his interest." *Parent of 15 year old girl*

The aim of the 'present' parent is to build up their teen's self-esteem to such a level that they externalise their father's actions, rather than internalise. There is no easy way to do this, but continually point out their positive traits ("You have loads of friends so there can't be anything wrong with you"), be extra gentle with them at vulnerable times and remind them how lucky you are to have them.

Feeling unloved by absent parent. When the absent parent moves away or becomes heavily distracted by a new family/partner, it is easy for their left-behind teen to feel unloved and unwanted. Sometimes, they will become insecure and wonder if and when you will get fed up with them too and stop loving them. This can manifest itself in challenging behaviour, designed to test your limits and see if you can be pushed away; they want to see if your love is conditional or whether you too will desert them when the going gets tough.

Persevere with the unconditional love, which does not mean that you have to accept unreasonable behaviour, and make it clear that you are around for the duration. Encourage them to talk to you about their dad (or mum) and how his actions make them feel. Don't rubbish their feelings in an attempt to discredit the ideas behind them (for example, "What nonsense – of course your dad loves you!").

Involved parent's feelings towards their ex-partner. It is likely that your feelings towards your ex are unequivocally negative (or, to put it bluntly, you hate the b*****d for what he is doing to your teen!). Yet, he is your child's parent and you may be torn between protecting your child and telling it like it is. Is it beneficial for your teen to know what a lying, cheating git their father is – or is it better to make excuses for him ("He is *very* busy at work and couldn't get here this weekend")?

The older they get, the less they will probably thank you for protecting their feelings. They want the truth, however unpalatable it is, and the sooner they get it, the sooner they can start absorbing the reality into their psyche. So it might be best to tell them the facts ("That was your father – he says that he is spending the weekend with his new girlfriend so can't see you as planned on Saturday") but try to keep your opinion and emotions out ("That was your good-for-nothing father – he says that he is spending the weekend yet again with his tarty new girlfriend so can't see you as planned on Saturday. Honestly, it's about time he got his priorities right and acted like a proper father."), and let them make up their own minds.

Teen's mixed emotions about absent parent. Your teen is likely to oscillate between hating their parent and loving them – in fact, they are likely to feel the same for you depending on whether you are currently in their good books or not. But, for the absent parent, they may have an extra layer of emotional complexity to contend with – that of assimilating their feelings towards the parent with their feelings towards you. Thus, for example, what happens if they are determined to make excuses for their errant parent and love them with protective fierceness, no matter what? How do they reconcile this with the knowledge that the father they love so much treated you so badly (or, indeed, treats them themselves badly)?

The resulting state of 'cognitive dissonance' means that the only way they can deal with the psychological discomfort is by changing one of the contradictory cognitions they hold about dad. This means that they can either stop loving him/accept he is less than perfect, or deny that he has *really* (or, at least, deliberately) done you any wrong. This may mean their minimising or discrediting your whole history, and this can be hard for you to swallow.

Again, it is probably best to let your confused teen work out their own feelings. Maybe they are in denial, but denial is the only way they can cope with the conflicting emotions surging through them. Try not to force through this wall of denial; let it happen at their own pace, when they are ready. Keep offering love and acceptance and let your child sort out their feelings when they have the maturity to do so.

"It can be very galling when the absent father is loved to death no matter what he has done either to the teen or the mother. My

daughter made up all sorts of excuses for his behaviour and I was left feeling like the big bad wolf. Somehow I kept my feelings to myself and she has now matured enough to see him for what he really is and has a great relationship with him." *Mother of teenage girl*

2 Involved 'absent' parent

Different difficulties can arise when the 'absent' parent is very much involved in your child's life. It could be that they have shared residency or that they have regular access. Both of these mean that your teen is likely to stay with their other parent at least one night a week, perhaps at weekends and probably half the school holidays. The other parent is likely to have access to communications from school, attend parents' evenings and events and otherwise be very involved in your teen's life.

Problems that can arise include the following:

- The contrast between the lifestyle offered by the other parent and your own. The other parent may be better off and be able to offer 'better' birthday presents, a bigger house or more expensive treats/activities.

- Parenting styles may well differ: one of you may be more relaxed with rules or simply have different rules or expectations with regard to behaviour, homework, clothes and other issues.

"My 15 year old stays with her dad Monday through to Wednesday. He is much more relaxed than me about things like homework and manners. I insist she does her homework before she watches TV, for example. And we always eat dinner together at the table – there she eats in front of the telly with a lap tray, which I hate. But my ex is far too strict, in my opinion, about her clothes. I let her wear typical teenage clothes because that's what they all wear. He seems to want to cover her up and make her look frumpy. It is hard for my daughter and for me. It's always "But my dad let's me do this ..." or "Dad won't let me wear this – it's not fair!" But she seems to understand that there are different rules in different houses and she generally accepts that." *Parent of a teenage girl*

■ Step-parents and step-siblings can complicate the situation. Your teen may resent their parent's new partner or perhaps you do and feel threatened by the affection your child holds for them. They may or may not get on with step-siblings (who may have their own issues of split families) and whose lives they have to slip in and out of. Grandparents and family occasions from each side can all make life even more complicated.

■ Finally, conflict can be especially intense when the teen's two parents cannot be civil to each other. When parents don't talk to each other and/or they compete for their child's affections, things can clearly get very tricky indeed. School events require complicated seating arrangements (and maybe doubling up at parents' evenings), notes sent home from school don't reach the other parent, parties get missed because of lack of communication ... and ' list goes on.

The key to all these difficulties is communication. It is tial to keep the lines of communication open between you your teen (see Chapter 3) and between you and your ex (e if you hate their guts). Teens are fairly adaptable and can accept living arrangements that would seem deeply unsettling to us adults, but the more they can share their feelings with you (or with somebody), the better. Keep the school fully informed of any difficult situations and try to minimise any possibilities of antagonising your ex-partner. Try not to take sides or make your teen feel disloyal for wanting to be with the other parent and make efforts not to avoid mentioning the other parent – let your teen tell you about what they did with their dad or what their dad's girlfriend said.

Extra help

A good place for your teen to go for extra support is **www.there4me.com** – a site run by the NSPCC for children aged 12-16 in the UK who are having difficulties.

If they want to talk to someone, they can call ChildLine on 0800 11 11 at any time of day or night, seven days a week. Lines are often busy, so keep trying.

A good website for parents and teens going through divorce is **www.divorceaid.co.uk/child/teenagers.htm** which has separate sections for teens and for parents.

Also try Parentline on their free 24-hour helpline: 0808 800 2222. Parentline Plus (which runs Parentline) is a government-funded initiative with trained volunteers to help with a range of problems that parents might be experiencing. It's also worth checking out their website at **www.parent lineplus.org.uk**

Lone parents can also contact Gingerbread, which is an

organisation run by and for lone parents, for emotional
support: 0800 018 4318, weekdays 10am to 3pm or their
website **www.gingerbread.org.uk**

Holidaying with your teenager

Let's face it, however healthy your relationship with your
child, many teens (and their parents) would rather undergo
root canal treatment with an unqualified dentist than endure
a family holiday. Yet sometimes needs must, so read on to find
out how to make it as enjoyable as possible for everyone.

First of all, involve them in the planning stage. Much of what
you would consider a fun time is likely to elicit yawns from
them (though they may secretly want to join in – it is not cool
to show enthusiasm for much beyond talking to their mates,
texting and computer games). You have to accept that their
idea of fun is different from your own. So, give them a pile of
brochures and a budget and ask them to come up with some
ideas. You mightn't accept all their ideas (for a start, Club 18-
30 won't let you in) but you could incorporate as many as you
can. This will give them a feeling of empowerment – instead
of being told what to do, they can feel involved in the decision-
making.

Once you set off, agree some ground rules about things like
texting friends back home, going off on their own, joining in
family activities/meals, drinking – and looking bored (only
allowed in the mornings, for example). A great way to engage
teens can be going to a place where they speak the lingo but
you don't. They are likely to really enjoy translating and being
relied upon by mum and dad!

Their first holiday without you

The trials and tribulations of them holidaying with you are nothing compared with the worry and anxiety of them holidaying without you. What age is it appropriate for them to do their own thing? Well, it depends on what that 'thing' is; organised holidays like adventure camps are suitable from pre-teen age (and younger) and this age might also go with a friend's family on their holiday (though you probably have to reciprocate by inviting the friend along on yours). But their first-ever holiday without adults probably happens around the age of 17/18 and could involve a Club 18-30, going with a boy/girlfriend or just a few mates booking a package to Tenerife.

Worrying about their safety, well-being and what they are getting up to when freed from the shackles of parental control is inevitable. Alcohol consumption, drugs and sexual activity are probably the main sources of anxiety for parents. Try and engage them with your concerns rather than lecture them; try to focus on the practical things they can do to keep themselves safe (always stay with a friend, be alert to drink spiking, get taxis together rather than walk, use condoms, ensure they have emergency phone numbers and credit cards for unforeseen problems) rather than say "Don't do it". Talk through scenarios that could happen ("What will you do if your mate cops off with someone leaving you by yourself in a club?" or "What would you do if your wallet was stolen?" and so on).

Remember this is a rite of passage (for both of you) and part of creating independent, assured and responsible adults.

Coping when they are learning to drive

Your 17 year old can't wait to get behind the wheel and nags you to take them out in the car and pay for lessons. You, on the other hand, have doubts about their maturity to handle such grown-up equipment (and worry about the cost of lessons). Yet, learning to drive is a vital step in your almost-adult's development. It is a life skill and if you cast doubts on their abilities you risk throwing their self-esteem out of synch. Far better to bite the bullet, grit your teeth and let them get on with it.

Many parents find it hard to teach their own kids to drive (maybe you could swap with a friend?) but you may have another family member who is willing to help. Ideally, they will have weekly lessons with a reputable and approved driving school backed up with regular practice sessions with someone else.

Try to stay calm while you are in the car with them. Panicking or shouting will only get them flustered and make them question their competence. Your job is to instil confidence, not continually shake your head in wonder that they haven't crashed yet. Use praise rather than criticism ("You handled that corner well" rather than "You missed the lamppost by inches!"). Don't contradict – or belittle – what they are being taught by the professionals as it will only confuse them.

When they finally fly the nest (if teens do any more)

While many parents might rejoice when their teen leaves home for university, college, gap year or the wonderful world of work, many others mourn this new stage and find the empty nest syndrome difficult to cope with. The house is suddenly quiet, the food in the fridge stays where you left it, the washing machine is on less often and, more significantly, your child's rite of passage serves to reflect your own inevitable aging process as you move into a new stage in life's journey.

Many mums (and dads) feel redundant, less valued, less needed and less busy as they struggle to fill the emotional gap in their lives, while plenty of others are just thrilled to get shot of their teens and start enjoying their freedom again. When your teen flies the nest it is a good idea to coincide their leaving with some (or all) of the following:

- Plan a trip – a holiday, weekend away, round the world trip, whatever your resources allow. Enjoy your new freedom!

- Take up a new hobby or interest that you have not had time to indulge in while the kids were at home.

- Do voluntary work with any spare time that you are now looking to fill.

- Look at new money-making ideas, increase your hours at work or start selling stuff on eBay (all the stuff your teen has left behind, perhaps?)

- Redecorate the house – including, perhaps, their old room (but bear in mind that teens, like boomerangs, often tend to return in vacations or when things get tough).

"Do not touch their room! My kids hate it when we change anything in the house when they are away. They seem to need the stability of the home they have left behind as most of them live in student chaos. We do of course do exactly what we want but we tell them now what is going on. Their room is definitely out of bounds beyond giving it a good clean." *Parent of teenager*

It is important, however you feel, to let go of your independent child. This means resisting the urge to ring them (too much), though the occasional text is usually OK, and never, ever 'pop round' uninvited (and definitely don't let yourself in with the spare key to 'tidy up').

Parenting at a distance – how to continue being a parent now they're gone

You can and should still be 'Mum' or 'Dad' even when your offspring no longer live at home. Parenting at a distance has different rules and these include the following:

- Be supportive – but at a distance. Agree a contact schedule that they are happy with. This may just evolve or you may want to discuss it in advance. Some teens are happy to speak to mum or dad every night – others would be horrified at that intrusion into their independence. Texts and emails are a good, less intrusive way to keep the lines of communication open.

- Show an interest – but not too much. It is fine to ask how their assignment went or a new date, but don't force the issue if they clearly don't want to discuss it. It is about being there when they do want to talk.

- Picking up the pieces when things go wrong. Some parents are secretly pleased to be needed again when their teen needs a shoulder to cry on. But resist the urge to make them dependent again – it is too easy to say '"Oh, poor you. Come back home to Mummy and I'll make sure you're OK". Encouraging their independence even in the face of hardship is a good lesson in life.

■ Learn to have less control. When our kids are little, we know exactly where they are and who they are with at all times. If we are uncomfortable with them doing an activity or going somewhere, we can easily say No. This sort of control over their lives gets weaker and weaker as they grow, but once they leave home, you have to accept that you have *no* control over them any more – which is, after all, probably why they are leaving home. If they want to stay out all night, walk home in the dark, take drugs or miss lectures, there is nothing you can realistically do about it. You have to accept that they are grown up and need to make their own choices; trust in them and in the values you have instilled and *let go*!

■ Financial support. How much (if at all) you are prepared to support them financially depends on their and your circumstances. If they are a student, see the next section. If they are working, should you bail them out if they fall behind with their rent? Should you buy them a car? Should you pay for special clothes such as outfits for weddings? Whatever you decide, try and justify your reasons against the need to help them stand on their own two feet – and be prepared to be consistent with all your children.

When they don't fly the nest

In the good old days children generally did leave home in their teens, but now it's not uncommon for children to stay at home well into their twenties – and beyond. In fact, you may be reading this and just yearning for your grown-up kids to finally flee the nest. The number of adults aged 20-25 living with their parents has increased by almost a third from 1991-2003 [figures from the Office of National Statistics]. It could also be that your teen did leave home but is now back like an errant homing pigeon, perhaps after their Gap year or if they are struggling to cope financially or they're finding the delights of processed ready meals not quite up to mum's cooking.

The big question is, should your teen pay 'rent' in these circumstances if they are working? Maybe. Perhaps. It depends on their and your situation. If they are saving for a deposit in a low-paid job and you are financially secure, it seems churlish to take their hard-earned cash off them for services you have been providing for free up to now.

But teens should certainly contribute to the household in some way, whether by having a set of regular chores or cooking the family meal one or two days a week. They should pay their own expenses, including mobile phone costs, and probably those little extras like picking up pizzas or chocolate Hobnobs on their way home from work. And they should definitely not be slamming doors any more.

Mind the Gap

The Gap year between school and university is now as much a part of most teenager's expectations and rights as having a mobile phone or iPod. Not only do they expect to have an exotic year out travelling the four corners of the earth or teaching English in Peru, but they think it is their rightful reward for working hard at school (where is our Gap year for working so hard at work?). Parents have to cope with a range of issues surrounding the Gap year:

The cost. Ideally they should fund their own extended holiday, but if you want them to do it safely (and who doesn't?), guess who will be footing the bill? So, you will pay airfares (to avoid their hitch-hiking), accommodation upgrades (so they stay in less dodgy areas), internet access (so they can reassure you that they are OK) and all the kit necessary to keep them healthy (water purification tables, personal injection kits and so on).

The worry. Oh, the worry. Will they be safe? Are they eating properly? Are they being sensible? Do they have access to washing facilities? Are they dating some unsavoury, unwashed fellow-trekker? Will they abandon their degree and never return?

It is probably impossible to offer reassuring words about such worries in a book such as this, but that won't stop us trying. Rest assured, dear Mum and Dad, that the overwhelming majority of Gappers come to no harm and return after their year a better, more rounded individual. The rare horror story that reaches the papers does so precisely because it is so rare. Be aware of falling victim to the 'availability heuristic', which is when sensationalised newspaper reports of rare events make those events seem much more likely to our anxious minds.

Having said that, a few basis precautions are sensible:

Discuss safety with your teenager before they go. Have safety codes in place, whereby they email a reliable person (such as you) or text you about where they are going and when they are expected back. Discuss stranger-danger, drugs, safe sex (yes, really) and food hygiene and make sure that they are as equipped to cope as possible. Work through well-thought-out plans and timetables and consider what could go wrong so that alternative plans can be developed. Make sure they see their GP about getting the necessary jabs before they set off. And, most importantly, if you are not already – get yourself online so you can stay in touch.

It is worthwhile getting hold of a book about taking a Gap year – your local bookshop shelves should be groaning under the weight of the many guides out there. There are plenty of websites too [try **www.gapyear.com** or **www.gapyeardirectory.co.uk**].

Remember that what they gain should outweigh your fears. And, when you casually mention to your colleagues at work that your teen is back-packing their way around Australia, you will feel nothing but pride (and, perhaps, envy).

Of course, travelling is not the only option for a year out. The year is also an opportunity to work and earn money, either to help with their bank balance when they go off to study or to pay for their dream trip later in the year. While any job will sometimes do, the Gap year gives once in a lifetime opportunities that your teen could be encouraged to explore. The Year in Industry is probably the best such scheme, with students able to earn between £8,000 and £12,000 if they work for a whole year. Additionally, many Year in Industry students gain sponsorship from the companies they work for during their time at university [**www.yini.org.uk**].

Other possibilities include Year out Drama, which provides drama courses for budding thespians [**www.yearoutdrama. com**], has links with the RSC and gives an opportunity to perform at the Edinburgh Festival, and Tante Marie, which gives students cookery skills and the opportunity to gain employment in the ski and travel industries [**www.tantemarie. co.uk**].

For a list of well-structured year out programmes that adhere to a clear code of practice, visit **www.yearoutgroup.org/ organisations.htm**. You can share this with your teen and ask them to consider which may be best for them if they need to cover their costs.

Your worries about their Gap year may be nothing compared to the worries that preoccupy the over-active minds of your teens, and the next chapter deals with all those fears and worries that are likely to be haunting them.

Chapter 9

9/11 and other worries and fears

According to recent research by the authors[28], the most common thing that teens worry about is their future. This includes such worries as what will happen to them if they fail their exams, if someone they love will die, whether they will ever get a boyfriend/girlfriend, whether they will get a good job when they leave school, and so on. Some worry about their future sexual relationship, Aids and pregnancy (see Chapter 7), while others worry about whether or not they will meet their parents' expectations (see below).

What do teens worry about?

According to the authors' previous research[28] the following are the issues that teenagers themselves say they worry about "a lot":

1 Their future, including school, exams, careers and health – 50%

2 Sexual issues – 44%

3 Bullying – 20%

4 Drugs – 15%

5 Death, including worries about family members dying – 10%

6 Gambling – 7%

We found that girls worried about sexual issues more than boys, but otherwise there were no gender differences. Peak 'worrying' age, we found to be age 13-15, except for worrying about the future, which did not fall after age 15.

What do parents think teenagers worry about? According to the research we carried out for this book, these are the top issues that parents believe their teens worry about:

1 Schoolwork/exams etc – 40%
2 Their appearance – 38%
3 Friends/fitting in etc – 32%
4 Money – 24%
5 Romantic relationships – 22%
6 Their future in general – 18%

In general, encouraging your teen to share their worries is a good starting point. However, just knowing what most kids worry about can give you an insight into what's going on inside their heads. If your teen is typical of everyone else's, you can pretty much assume that they worry about the same sort of things. Some of these worries are addressed in other chapters and sections of this book.

Worrying about their future career is a top concern and probably one that can be addressed by you to some extent. Talk to them regularly about their career aspirations, but don't put pressure on them to either have any aspirations or to have particular career goals. Children may feel under pressure to pursue professional careers like their parents, and worry about not meeting these expectations. Even children whose parents don't have high-powered jobs may be under pressure to be, for example, the first in their family to go to university. Fear of not meeting parental expectations can cause 'self-handicapping', which means that they subconsciously sabotage their chances so that the feared failure is not attributable to their lack of ability: for example, if they don't complete assignments or fail to revise for exams, then they can blame their subsequent failure on that rather than any inability on their part. This is a way of protecting their fragile egos – it is better for them that everybody thinks they didn't study hard enough than they weren't capable.

Coping with the aftermath of terrorist atrocities – dealing with the 'will it happen to me?' question

9/11. The London Tube bombs. The Boxing Day Tsunami. New Orleans Flood. Hurricanes, tornados, earthquakes … these are all events that that have pierced the consciousness of the public across the world. At these times, pictures of devastation, death and human suffering dominate the media and it is almost impossible for our teens to be immune to the effects.

Many of their reactions to these cataclysmic events are not dissimilar to our own: could it happen to us? How would we cope? Is the world a safe place? Will our lives ever be the same again? How can people do such terrible things to other people? Why is the world so unjust?

Addressing these tricky questions (and let's face it, philosophers have been wrestling with these since time immemorial) can at first glance appear rather intimidating, and may invoke the 'ostrich response'. However, they will not go away. Unfortunately, despite our best efforts, we don't have the answers. But what we do have is some strategies to help you to help your teen come to terms with such atrocities in the world:

- **Exposure to the media.** For many parents, the first dilemma is how much to allow your teen to see. TV news reports can be very graphic and there is a temptation to shelter your child. Obviously it depends on the age (it will be impossible to shelter older teens) and sensitivity of your child, but you have to bear in mind that these things will be discussed in the playground. Sheltering them completely is probably not a realistic approach. It is probably better to accept that such images will be difficult to avoid so sitting down to watch with them (where possible) may be a wiser choice. This enables them to raise any questions and concerns that they may have – although whether you can actually answer them is another matter.

- **Fostering an open environment.** This is about creating an atmosphere in which your teen feels comfortable raising their concerns and fears but without feeling pressured to do so. Sometimes you have to wait until they are ready to talk, and that could be at a time when you least expect it, for example, while you're loading the dishwasher or washing the car. It may be a good idea, when such events dominate the news, for you to try and be around a bit more than usual so that if and when the urge to talk takes

them, you are there. However, try not to put pressure on
them by demanding that they tell you how they feel.

■ **Don't feel as though you have to have all the answers.**
As parents, up to now, your teen may have viewed you as
an 'all-seeing, all-knowing' parent who was able to deal
with any problems that might arise. However, sometimes
there are no answers, and either lying, or just giving glib
responses, will not cut the mustard. Your integrity is
much more likely to stay intact if you admit that you are
struggling with the issues too. This may come as a shock
to them, and feel uncomfortable to you, but actually it is
an important developmental stage for both of you. You
can still be an effective parent without having all the
answers and your kids will probably respect you more in
the long term for your honesty.

■ **Put things in perspective.** It is very hard at such
an emotive time to be objective about the risks but it
may be your role as a parent to try to do so. Remind your
children how many planes fly each day/month/year without crashing; or how many tube journeys are accom-
plished without incident. Humans are irrational creatures
and can be subject to flawed reasoning. For example, the
so-called 'availability heuristic' means that if we can call
to mind an event more easily, then we think it is more
likely to happen. This is why parents tend to overestimate
the risks of child abduction, which is actually quite rare,
but the headlines about the tragic Hollys and Jessicas
mean that such fears are more readily available in our
minds.

Fear of being attacked

Our survey said...

Fear of their teenager being attacked was the top worry for parents in our survey, with 29% citing this as their main concern.

Regrettably, this is not an unrealistic fear. A survey carried out by Victim Support in 2002 showed that a quarter of young people said they had been the victim of crime, whether it was theft, mugging, violent attack or even, more rarely, sexual assault. The best way to tackle such fears is to help your teen feel safe. The following are sensible tips to share with your teen:

- Always try to go places with a friend, whether to the shopping mall or walking to school.

- Tell people where you are and when you will be back. Never go off anywhere without informing someone so they know when you are expected back. A quick text to mum or dad is ideal.

- Keep valuables such as iPods and mobile phones out of sight and don't walk along speaking on your phone or listening to your iPod. Apart from exposing these items, you make yourself vulnerable by being unable to hear someone approach.

- When you walk on the pavements, face oncoming traffic so you won't be surprised by someone pulling up behind you.

- If you are uneasy about someone when out and about, nip into a shop, cross the road or seek help. The best people to approach in a public place are a family group – someone with children of their own.

- Never accept lifts from people you don't know very well. If you are unsure, ring your parent to check.

- Always carry emergency money with you, preferably hidden out of sight (and not in your purse/wallet).

- On buses or public transport, sit near the driver if the place is very quiet.

- Don't fight back if someone does try to nick your stuff.

- If you are home alone, don't tell strangers who ring up that no one is home. It is better to say that mum is in the bath than that she is out.

- Always check who is at the door before you answer it; ask them or look through an upstairs window. If you are not sure, ask them to come back later.

Dealing with death in the family

According to the Childhood Bereavement Trust (see end of this section) the majority of young people will be bereaved of someone close to them by the time they are 16. There is probably little that you can do to make things better if someone close to them is dying or has passed away. But you can help them cope with their feelings and help them with their grieving process. Parents often want to protect their children so may not tell them the truth about illness and survival expectancy.

Depending on their age and maturity, honesty may be the best policy, especially if they can see that other family members seem to know more than they do (this can lead to mistrust and resentment).

Teenagers are likely to feel the same or similar emotions as adults when they learn of a death in their family. These feelings can range from numbness (not feeling anything, being unable to cry or express their grief 'appropriately'), denial (appearing to carry on with their lives as though nothing has happened), anger (why did this happen?), depression (I can't go on without this person), confusion (what will happen now?) and guilt (I should have been nicer/spent more time with them – or even guilt at enjoying themselves, laughing or having fun over the next few weeks).

These feelings are all normal and natural and it helps to encourage your teen to talk to you or someone else about how they feel. Make it clear to them that there is no 'expected' way to grieve and that it is fine if they feel angry, if they don't cry, if they want to be alone, if they want to be with their friends – in fact, whatever helps them cope should be OK.

Bereavement can shake the faith of adults, but for children this may be their first encounter with the dawning understanding that the world is not always a good and just place. "It's not fair" is a common rant and, of course, they are right. But whereas more worldly adults know that life isn't always fair, this realisation can come as a shock to teenagers. This can shake their entire world, their belief in good and evil, justice and punishment. If you have religious faith, it is likely that your teenager may rage against God or appear to lose faith in their religion. Accept this as part of the grieving process and try to avoid giving glib responses (such as "It's all for the best" or "God works in mysterious ways"). It is better to admit that the world is an unfathomable place at times and that everyone has to work out their own understanding of the meaning of life (and what, if anything, follows).

Dealing with questions about death, the after-life and the soul, will depend on what you yourself believe. It is probably wise to answer as best you can with differing views so that they can pick one that seems right to them. Rather than categorically state that there is nothing after death (which can be very hard to deal with), it is better to say that some people believe souls carry on somewhere (although you could add that you are not so sure that they do). They will spend their lifetime working out the answers to these difficult conundrums themselves, just as we have all had to (and still do, probably).

As far as the practicalities are concerned, it is probably a good idea to explain funeral arrangements in advance so they are prepared. If there is a ceremony at a crematorium, or a religious ceremony at a church, mosque or synagogue, explain what will happen. If you belong to a religious faith, it is essential to explain rituals in advance; it can be alarming to see the bereaved sitting on low chairs, with their clothes cut at a Jewish Shiva if they have never experienced this before. Of course, if your teenager does not want to take part in the rituals (or even attend the funeral), it is probably wise not to force them. Similarly, if they do want to attend, there is probably no good reason for trying to prevent this; trying to protect them from too much distress is unlikely to help them in the long term.

The question of how much time to take off school will probably arise. There is no stock answer as it depends on the child, their relationship with the bereaved and, most importantly, how they feel. Sending them to school when their hearts and minds are elsewhere can seem like a kind thing to do (to distract them) but could be cruel and stressful for them. Be guided by them – some will want to return to the comfort of familiar routines and friends as soon as possible while others may take longer. They may encounter insensitive comments at school (not just from their peers but from teachers too) or may be otherwise distraught by seemingly innocuous events in the classroom (such as reading certain things). This is all normal but do consider talking to a teacher or Year Head if things get out of hand.

Adjusting in the long term to a family bereavement is as hard for teenagers as for anyone. Christmas, birthdays and all the usual milestones must be passed without the missing person. The first year is always the hardest as they experience these events for the first time without their loved one, so take extra care in arrangements for these occasions. Perhaps consider going away for Christmas or having a new family (who don't normally come at Christmas) visit to make the empty armchair less noticeable. Talk about your loved one – don't feel that you should avoid the issue for fear of bringing all their feelings to the surface again. It is healthier to have them on the surface than buried, and a healthy grieving process should culminate in comfort discussing the relative who died.

When, however, does normal, healthy grieving turn into something more worrying? Some of the signs to watch out for include:

- Use of maladaptive (unhealthy) coping techniques such as drugs (see Chapter 10 for signs), comfort eating and alcohol.

- Missing school or grade-dropping.

- Aggressive outbursts.

- Long spells of weeping, refusal to get out of bed, loss of interest in hobbies and friends.

- Refusal to mention the relative who died.

If you are worried about how your teen is coping, contact the Child Bereavement Trust [**www.childbereavement.org.uk**] for some useful advice. Or try the Childhood Bereavement Network [**www.childhoodbereavementnetwork.org.uk**]. For teenagers who have to cope with the death of a sibling The Compassionate Friends [**www.tcfsiblingsupport.org.uk**] has been recommended by one parent who we surveyed for this book.

Worries about humanitarian issues

As young people meander through the transition from child to adult, they become more aware of the environment outside their own little world. Young children are very egocentric; they believe that the world revolves around them and that nothing of importance exists beyond their cosy existence. As they grow up they may still try to get the world to revolve around them but become increasingly aware that there is a whole society out there that exists away from them.

Added to this is the increasing prominence that young people tend to give to issues of justice and fairness, and you begin to see why teenagers can get embroiled in global humanitarian issues that many, more-world-weary adults simply shrug their shoulders at. Teenagers, bless 'em, are naïve enough to think they can change the world and really 'make poverty history' while their cynical parents may not even bother trying to make a difference (so, thank goodness for teenagers!).

Another explanation for adolescent zeal for humanitarian causes is that they are still trying to find their identity and discover who they really are. Attaching themselves firmly to a (fashionable) worthwhile cause tells them and others that they must be a caring individual who is passionate about important issues. Hence, teenagers might well harangue you about vegetarianism, recycling, climate change and boycotting less ethical companies. And it is probably a good thing that they do feel so passionate. Many changes are wrought through the enthusiasm and righteous indignation of our teenagers, so three cheers for them (except when they sneer at you for enjoying a roast or they bully you into changing coffee brand).

Coping with their current fad (oh, such a patronising word – don't let them see this) should incorporate the following:

- Don't ever call their passion for green issues or animal rights a 'fad' (we never would!).

- Respect their views; this means listening to them and not rubbishing them.

- Resist the temptation to continually point out the flaws in their arguments or to gleefully point out lapses in their dedication ("Ha – but you're wearing leather shoes!").

- Challenging them gently is OK and probably useful for

their developing awareness, but don't ridicule their arguments.

■ Don't threaten them to change their beliefs. If you refuse to let them eat a veggie diet, they are likely to cling to their desire to refuse meat even more (the theory of psychological reactance means that if you restrict people's freedom, they will react strongly to do what is restricted to them).

■ If they want to change their diet, perhaps to become vegetarian or vegan, it is probably sensible to facilitate this by providing a suitable alternative (or better still, get them to cook their own). Make sure their diet is still balanced and healthy and get advice from organisations such as the Vegetarian Society [**www.vegsoc.org**]. More restrictive diets, like lactose-free, should only be undertaken with medical supervision.

All these concerns pale into insignificance, however, when you encounter the really big issues that can keep you awake at night. Read on – if you dare!

Chapter 10

Drugs, eating disorders and other worries that keep you awake at night

It's a teenager's job to keep you awake at night, but occasionally there may be more to disrupt your sleep than usual. This chapter addresses some of your scarier nightmares.

Our survey says...

Our survey of 170 parents suggests that their top worries about their teenagers are:

1 Their personal safety/being attacked – 29%
2 School/exams – 27%
3 Their future/careers etc – 22%
4 Peer pressure/drugs – 17%
5 Getting in with the wrong crowd – 17%
6 Their health – 15%
7 Their happiness – 13%

Drugs

Humans have been using chemicals to alter the way they feel for hundreds, if not thousands, of years but there are three main areas in which your teenager can cross the line between substance use and abuse:

■ If their drug of choice is illegal

■ If their use of it is adversely affecting their health, education, social life or well-being

■ If their use of the substance leads them to take part in other illegal or anti-social activities (such as stealing to fund a habit or causing public disturbances when drunk)

Of the legal drugs, tobacco and alcohol are the most commonly used by teens. According to a BUPA website [**www.hcd2. bupa.co.uk**], where you can download a Teens and Drugs factsheet, almost a quarter of 15 year olds smoke regularly, and 85% of teenagers who smoke become addicted. About a third of teenagers aged 13-17 drink at least once a week (including alcopops). Solvents, whose fumes are inhaled to give a high, include glue and lighter refills. In terms of illegal drugs, BUPA point out that almost a third of 15 year olds have tried an illegal drug, usually cannabis, at some point.

Interestingly, another piece of research (for Frank, the drugs helpline, see help box at end of chapter) suggests that around 20% of teenagers in 2004 faked drug-use in order to fit in with their mates.

Why do teenagers take drugs?

Here are some reasons from our own research[28] that teenagers give for experimenting with drugs:

- To be 'cool'
- Because my friends are
- To fit in
- Curiosity
- Because it is illegal (to rebel)
- To get high
- To stop me thinking about my problems
- Because I get stressed

How do I know if my teen is using substances?

The simple answer is that you might not know until they have a problem (see below). It is hard to know if your child has started experimenting with a substance until they are abusing it and things are starting to get out of hand. Signs of a problem include:

- Sudden lethargy or changes in sleeping habits
- Moodiness or mood swings (over and beyond normal teenage behaviour)
- Aggression
- Secretiveness
- Seeming 'spaced out' or not all there
- Stealing money
- Appetite change
- Different social groups
- Dropping old hobbies and interests

Many of these signs could be signs of other issues such as bullying (see Chapter 6) or just plain old hormones. The only way you can know for sure is probably by asking them – but they are not necessarily going to admit it. Going through their room or reading their diary should be a last resort strategy as this will invoke a serious breach of trust that may be difficult to recover from.

What to do if you suspect your child has a substance abuse problem?

The most effective strategy is to talk to them. It is tempting to rant and rage, to ground them or stop their pocket money, but these are short-term strategies that are unlikely to be effective in the medium or long term. Your focus should be about them staying safe and about the risks and consequences of their actions; trying to coerce them into stopping is not likely to work.

If your child is abusing substances, they started doing this for a reason and you need to tackle this too. Perhaps they feel stressed and over-burdened at school – just telling them to quit smoking cannabis will not deal with this problem. Helping them deal with their problems in a more constructive way is essential if they are to drop the bad habits.

You may also have to accept that your perception of a problem might not be the same as theirs. If they take ecstasy when out clubbing, this may be alarming for you but part of normal club life for them. Trying to get them to stop something they enjoy is not easy; using scare stories has not been proven effective because of the 'representativeness bias': teenagers are far more likely to be influenced by the fact that all their mates take drugs with no ill effects than by a story in the newspaper of one girl who died from it. It is far better, for example, to help them 'use' safely (eat first, drink water, make sure you have a pre-arranged means of getting home) than to try to stop it happening.

It is useful to be armed with accurate information (see box at end of chapter) to give your child and also to encourage your teen to seek out their own information, help or advice. Remember that a bit of experimenting is probably normal for teenagers – your job is to try to limit this within safe boundaries.

It is worth pointing out here that some parents might be quite tolerant of their teenagers using some drugs, such as smoking tobacco or even cannabis. Some readers may well have done this themselves (and may still indulge) so be wondering what the fuss is about. Whether you approve or not is personal choice but arm yourself with the facts first. The dangers of cigarette smoking are well-documented but not everyone is convinced that cannabis is harmful. Check out the facts and do your research. Remember that more is known about its ill-effects than when you might have started smoking the weed. Also, there are new dangers linked with it now, such as stronger blends and associated access to harder drugs.

Gambling problems

There are more opportunities than ever for teenagers (and adults) to get involved in gambling. The proliferation of fruit machines, lottery scratchcards (for over 16s) and, more recently, online poker rooms (although technically illegal for under 18s to play) have all contributed to the ease with which teenagers can try out this potentially expensive pastime. According to the website **www.gamcare.org.uk**, research has shown that teenagers are three times more likely to develop a gambling addiction than adults.

Teenagers probably get into gaming or gambling for similar reasons to adults; for escapism, stress relief, the glamour and for the excitement that a big win promises. Of course, like adults, much of the time this can be a harmless activity; according to Connexions, 75% of teenagers gamble (see page 166) yet most don't become addicts. If your teen likes to 'play the slots' ask yourself (or your teen) the following questions:

- Do they miss school in order to gamble?

- Do they beg, borrow or even steal money to fund their habit?

- Do they ever use lunch money for gambling?

- Do they ever have to walk home because they have used their bus money gambling?

- Do they lie to you about their whereabouts?

If there are more Yes answers than No, then it is time to take your teen's playing seriously. According to GamCare [**www.gamcare.org.uk**], most problem gamblers develop their habit in their early teens; they point out that teenagers are attracted to adult activities but have not yet learned the responsibility that goes with the power of money. So, if your child has a problem with gambling, they are not alone.

Teenagers and gambling

A survey reported by Connexions [**www.connexions-cw. co.uk**] of 12-15 year olds found:

- 75% had played fruit/slot machines
- 47% had played scratchcards
- 40% had played the lottery draw
- 7% had been illegally sold tickets
- 5% showed signs of gambling addiction

The lonely or shy teen – when to really worry

Many parents rejoice if their teenagers are outgoing and popular and worry if they are excessively shy or appear lonely. We all want our kids to be happy and this is the real key between healthy shyness and the kind of shyness that is preventing them from enjoying their lives. Ask yourself (or your teen) these questions:

- Does your teen have one or more friends?

- Do they ever have friends round?

- Do they go to friends' houses?

- Do they go out every so often with friends?

- Do they talk about friends at school?

- Are they involved in the occasional social activity (e.g. a sport) even if they prefer solitary activities?

- Do they belong to any clubs or after-school activities?

- Do they go to social events if invited?

- Do they get invited to parties?

If there are more Yes answers than No, you probably need not worry, especially if they seem happy. Some teenagers (and adults) are happier with their own company and don't need a lot of friends. Introverts are thought to have a lower need for stimulation and it could just be that your teen fits this personality profile. Accept it and don't try to push them into doing things that they don't want to do.

If, however, your teen seems to have no real friends, rarely has people round or visits their houses, rarely goes out socially, doesn't mention any of their peers from school, rarely gets invited to anything and resists any attempts to get involved in social activities, then your teen may have a problem, possibly a form of social phobia. There may be reasons for their reluctance to engage; perhaps they are very self-conscious about their appearance (overweight, dental braces, acne etc) or perhaps they worry excessively about 'saying the wrong thing'. Psychologists who treat social phobias tend to help their clients challenge their distorted thinking (e.g. "Everyone is looking at me!") and replace it with more realistic statements ("Everyone is more concerned with themselves than with what I am doing"). The list on page 168 shows some other examples of how distorted thinking can be replaced with more accurate self-talk.

Distorted thoughts	Accurate replacement
I might do something stupid	So what – who cares? Everyone will just get on with their lives.
Everyone is talking about me.	Maybe for a few minutes until they move on to something better.
Everyone is laughing at me	If I look around I can see that they are not, actually.
I bet everyone thinks my . clothes are naff	I am dressed as I want to be and am comfortable – it is no one else's concern.

As well as challenging their distorted thinking, you should encourage your shy teenager to take small steps. There is little point pushing them to attend a party or a big event but start small; this process is what psychologists call 'desensitisation'; they start with small, manageable steps and build up to bigger challenges. So, your teen might start off going to some event with you, such as a family party, or going to a school club that only has a few members.

Finally, think about their social skills. Suggest opening phrases and small-talk ideas. Help them stand tall and talk to them about the importance of eye contact.

Shy and lonely teenagers can benefit from the opportunities afforded by new technologies, so encourage them to use chatrooms and develop email penpals, but talk to them about cybersafety issues first (see page 169).

Keeping safe on the internet

Teach your teen cybersafety with chatrooms, networking sites (such as MySpace and Bebo) and emailing. They should never:

- Give their true identity, address, phone number etc in chatrooms or to strangers.

- Send pictures of themselves to someone they don't know.

- Travel alone to meet someone they know only via the Internet.

- Talk about sexual issues with strangers, or engage in 'cybersex' (whereby they are asked to touch themselves etc)

- Put personal details on websites (e.g. MySpace)

If they ever feel uncomfortable they should ask an adult or just log off. Remind them that the person they are talking to could be anyone, and not the 15 year old boy they claim to be. Check out the following websites for more advice:

- BBC parenting at **www.bbc.co.uk/parenting/your_kids/ safety_internet.shtml**

- Chatsafe, an initiative run by Thames Valley Police: **www.thamesvalley.police.uk/chatsafe**

- GetNetWise is a public service offered by a coalition of internet industry corporations and offers excellent advice, including specific age-related sections: **www.kids.getnet-wise.org**

Eating disorders – signs and strategies (and not just in girls)

There are two main categories of eating disorders, anorexia and bulimia, and neither is really just about the desire to be thin; the issues are far more complex than that. Teenagers develop eating disorders because of control issues, because of unhappiness, or poor self-esteem or lack of confidence. Sometimes, teenagers feel that their lives are so out of control that restricting their food intake is the only thing that is within their control. Others get a boost to their fragile self-esteem by proving that they can be 'good' at something (losing weight). Some start off by wanting to look thinner, perhaps because they want to be more popular or more attractive, and start to get a buzz as the weight falls off. Many teens with eating disorders are 'body dysmorphic' which means that they see fat when they are really stick-thin.

Signs of eating disorders to watch out for include:

- Giving regular excuses for missing meals ("I've already eaten at a friend's" etc).

- Lack of enthusiasm about food.

- Strong reluctance to eat any 'fattening' foods.

- Going to the toilet after meals to vomit.

- Excessive exercise such as walking to school, jogging before school, using exercise equipment for hours.

In our own research (Mann et al 1995) we found that around 11% of girls we asked skipped meals 'quite often or very often' in order to lose weight. Only 40% of boys and 22% of girls said they were happy with their weight. When we repeated the research in 2004, we found that a quarter of girls we asked were unhappy with their weight and 16% of boys. Although the percentage of girls claiming to skip meals 'often' in order to lose weight has stayed stable across both research projects, the incidences of boys doing this seems to be rising; less than 2% of boys in 1995 but 8% in 2004.

According to the National Centre for Eating Disorders (see box at end of chapter), the average age for anorexia is 16 years. By age 15, one in three teenagers has been on a diet of some kind.

If you suspect your teenager has an unhealthy attitude (but not a full-blown eating disorder) towards food, their self-image, dieting etc, the following are some useful tips:

■ Say positive things about their appearance; don't lie, but compliment them regularly in order to build up their self-esteem.

■ Avoid comments about their weight, your weight or those of other people. This means not making disparaging remarks about yourself or others. It also means being careful not to praise friends for losing weight in front of your teen.

■ Restrict your own dieting behaviour; model healthy eating but avoid being obsessive about it. Encourage unhealthy treats sometimes too.

If you think your child does have an eating disorder there are various ways that you can get them help. The National Centre for Eating Disorders offers self-help programmes (at a cost) and there are a range of books available in bookshops to advise you (see the box at the end of this chapter). You should also speak to your GP about getting your child referred to specialist centres in severe cases.

Self harm – signs and strategies

According to The Samaritans, approximately 24,000 teenagers were admitted to Accident and Emergency for self-harm in England and Wales in 1998 (reported on BBC website: **www.bbc.co.uk/radio1/onelife/health/healthy_mind/ selfharm.shtml**).

Self-harm can include a range of behaviours from cutting the skin, pulling hair, burning the skin, or hitting the body against something or into something. Like many other symptoms, self-harm is a maladaptive (i.e. harmful) coping mechanism for dealing with stress or emotional pain. Self-harmers use the real pain they inflict as a way to distract themselves from their emotional distress. It can also be a cry for help, a dramatic way of drawing attention to their problems.

It can be immensely distressing and shocking for a parent to discover that their child is self-harming. You may notice signs of injuries that seem hard to explain away – cuts to the arms or wrists, bandages or plasters. Your child may cover up their body even in the warmest weather and be generally unhappy, depressed or moody.

If you come across an injury that your child has self-inflicted, stay calm and focus on sorting out the immediate first-aid issues (treat as you would any other injury). They are likely to be reluctant to admit their self-harm, but gentle questioning may draw them out. Try to hide your shock or revulsion and start the slow process to recovery. This will involve trying to help your teenager (and yourself) understand why they are self-harming and looking for ways of both treating the problem (i.e. looking for alternative ways of expressing their distress: SelfharmUK has some excellent suggestions including rubbing ice or using felt tip and flicking elastic bands on their wrists) and treating the symptoms (looking at what is causing their distress). Check out the info box at the end of this chapter – you don't need to do this without support.

When your child steals

It is likely that many teenagers will, at some point, steal something, but this does not necessarily make them career criminals. They may steal for a 'dare', for the thrill or to impress their mates. Regular or frequent stealing in teens is a cause for concern, if only because they are likely to end up with a criminal record that could scupper their future goals. You will need to stay calm (as always, but easier said than done) and try to ascertain why they are stealing.

Stealing to get things they want is probably more of a concern than stealing for other reasons as it may reflect a poorly developed sense of right and wrong at this age. Stealing because they are angry, to impress their mates, for the thrill of it, to get attention, or even to fund drug-habits – these are all underlying reasons that give you something to work with (though probably not on your own – you will need professional input).

Extra help

Solvent abuse. Call the Re-Solv national helpline on 01785 810762 or go to **www.re-solv.org/young_people.htm**

Parents Against Drug Abuse (PADA) was set up 15 years ago and provides good information about various substances: **www.btinternet.com/~padahelp**

www.dare.uk.com is a useful site for information about drugs and substances.

Finally, Frank is a great website for parents and teenagers to get up to date information about drugs

www.talktofrank.com. They have a helpline too: 0800 77 66 00

Gambling. The charity GamCare has a helpline, 0845 6000 133 and website **www.gamcare.org.uk**

Eating disorders. Your first port of call should probably be the Eating Disorders Association, which has a helpline for young people – 0845 634 7650 – and a website with pages for young people – **www.edauk.com**

Also try the National Centre for Eating Disorders at www.eating-disorders.org.uk

The BBC website is also well worth a visit: **www.bbc.co.uk/health/conditions/mental_health/ disorders_eating.shtml**

Self-harm. The website of the official National Inquiry into Young People and Self-harm, which launched March 2004 is **www.selfharmuk.org**.

Self Injury UK is an online support group for people of any age who self-injure:
http://health.groups.yahoo.com/group/siuk/

Information about self-harm and resources for those who are affected by the issue of deliberate self-harm among young people – **www.selfharm.org.uk**.

Endnote

This book necessarily focuses on the problems and difficulties that are part of life with a teenager. However, we want to stress that it is not all bad and that most teens come through this turbulent time as loving and mature adults (the state of their parents, of course, is another matter!). We were greatly reassured by the finding from our research that most parents felt that, on balance, they actually had a very good relationship with their teens (and this is before reading this book). Eighty-nine percent of respondents felt that their teenagers' relationship with their mum was 'good' or 'very good'. It is slightly less for dads at 80% but this is still a reassuring count. So be assured, you must be doing something right!

References

[1,2,3] Olweus, D (1978, 1980, 1991) in Bullying at School (1993), Oxford: Blackwell.

[4] Neary A and Joseph S (1994) Peer Victimization and Its Relationship to Self-Concept and Depression Among Schoolgirls. Personality and Individual Differences, v16 n1 p183-86 J.

[5] Bjorkqvist K, Lagerspetz KMJ, Kaukainen A (1992), Do Girls Manipulate and Boys Fight? Developmental Trends in Regard to Direct and Indirect Aggression, Aggressive Behavior, Vol 18 pp.117-27.

[6] Drake JA, Price JH, Telljohann SK, & Funk JB (2003). Teacher Perceptions and Practices Regarding School Bullying Prevention. Journal of School Health, 63, 347–355.

[7] MacLeod M, Morris S Why Me? Children Talking to ChildLine About Bullying. London: ChildLine, 1996.

[8] Smith P, Pepler D and Rigby K (Eds) (2004) Bullying in Schools: How Successful Can Interventions Be? Cambridge: University Press.

[9] Sullivan K, Cleary M and Sullivan G (2004) Bullying in Secondary Schools. London: Paul Chapman Publications.

[10] Media's Impact on Adolescents' Body Dissatisfaction',

Hofschire, L.J. & Greenberg, B.S. in 'op cit.' p146-147.

[11] 'Physiological Processes – What role do they play in the transition to adolescence?' Paikoff RL & Brooks-Gunn J, in 'From Childhood to Adolescence – A Transitional Period?', Montemayor et al Ed., Sage, London, 1990 p71-72

[12] op cit p73

[13] op cit p75

[14] The Nature of Adolescence. 2nd Ed.', Coleman JC and Hendry L, Routledge, London 1990

[15] Young People, Health and Family Life, Brannen J et al, OU Press, Buckingham, 1994, p178

[16] Social Exclusion report on teenage pregnancy, June 1999 **www.socialexclusion.gov.uk/downloaddoc.asp?id=69**

[17] ICM research commissioned by Teachers' TV for The Big Debate: Sex in the Classroom 2006 **www.teachers.tv/node/17595**.

[18] ibid

[19] 'The Adolescent in the Family', Noller P, and Callan V, Routledge, London, 1991 p48

[20] Risk, Gender and Youthful Bodies, Bunton R et al in Young People, Risk and Leisure – constructing identities in everyday life, Mitchell W et al Eds, Palgrave Macmillan, Basingstoke, 2004. p170-171

[21] op cit p172-3

[22] Risk-takers – Alcohol, Drugs, Sex and Youth, Plant M & Plant M, Routledge, London 1992. p100

[23] Sources of Sex Education Amongst Early Adolescents, Thornburg, HD, Journal of Early Adolescence, 1, 1980, p171-184.

[24] Adolescence, 10th Ed., Santrock JW, McGraw-Hill, New York, 2005, p260.

[25] Shaking the Tree of Knowledge for Forbidden Fruit: Where adolescents learn about sexuality and contraception, Sutton MJ et al in Sexual Teens, Sexual Media – investigating media's influence on adolescent sexuality, Brown JD et al, Lawrence Erlbaum, London, 2002 p34

[26] Sex and Relationship Education Guidance, DfEE, Nottingham, 2000, p25.

[27] The Choreography of Condom Use: How, not just if, young people use condoms, Hatherall B, Stone N, Ingham R & McEachran J, Brook, Southampton, 2005

[28] Mann S, Shaw M and Wineberg J (1995) Through Their Eyes.

Contact us

You're welcome to contact White Ladder Press if you have any questions or comments for either us or the author. Please use whichever of the following routes suits you.

Phone 01803 813343 between 9am and 5.30pm

Email enquiries@whiteladderpress.com

Fax 01803 813928

Address White Ladder Press, Great Ambrook, Near Ipplepen, Devon TQ12 5UL

Website www.whiteladderpress.com

What can our website do for you?

If you want more information about any of our books, you'll find it at **www.whiteladderpress.com**. In particular you'll find extracts from each of our books, and reviews of those that are already published. We also run special offers on future titles if you order online before publication. And you can request a copy of our free catalogue.

Many of our books also have links pages, useful addresses and so on relevant to the subject of the book. You'll also find out a bit more about us and, if you're a writer yourself, you'll find our submission guidelines for authors. So please check us out and let us know if you have any comments, questions or suggestions.

Index